More praise for *Polite Lies*

"Reading Kyoko Mori's *Polite Lies*, one makes a luminous journey into a woman's thoughts, hopes, memories, and experiences. Along her unpredictable paths, we see with her eyes, we hear with her ears, and we feel with her heart. It's a lovely and memorable trip."

—Shirlee Taylor Haizlip
Author of the bestselling *The Sweeter the Juice*

"Intensely honest and poignantly revealing . . . A courageous and remarkably nuanced piece of writing that reveals a great deal about Mori's native land of Japan and almost as much about her adoptive home of Wisconsin."

—*Madison Capital Times*

"Mori's exquisite language leads readers to an understanding of a civilization as highly developed as ours but one that has developed much differently in the area of human relations."

—*Booklist*

"This engagingly insightful discussion from one who has intimately experienced the two cultures is full of revelations about both."

—*Publishers Weekly*

"Powerful . . . Mori examines the way truth is circumvented in America and in her native Japan."

—*Kirkus Reviews*

ALSO BY KYOKO MORI

The Dream of Water

One Bird

Shizuko's Daughter

Polite Lies

Polite Lies

ON BEING A WOMAN CAUGHT
BETWEEN CULTURES

Kyoko Mori

Fawcett Books
The Ballantine Publishing Group
New York

A Fawcett Book
Published by The Ballantine Publishing Group

Portions of chapter twelve, "Home," appeared in
The Hungry Mind Review.

"The Retrieval System" (excerpt) copyright © 1978 by Maxine
Kumin, from *Selected Poems 1960–1990* by Maxine Kumin.
Reprinted by permission of W. W. Norton & Company, Inc.

http://www.randomhouse.com/BB/

Library of Congress Catalog Card Number: 98-96969

ISBN: 0-449-00428-7

This edition published by arrangement with Henry Holt and
Company, Inc.

Cover photo by Simon Metz
Text design by Betty Lew

Manufactured in the United States of America

First Fawcett Edition: April 1999

10 9 8 7 6 5 4 3 2

In memory of my aunts,

Akiko Mori and Keiko Nagai Maeshiba, and

June, the bodhisattva cat

Contents

Polite Lies

CHAPTER ONE

LANGUAGE

❋

When my third grade teacher told us that the universe was infinite and endless, I wrote down her words in my notebook, but I did not believe her. An endless universe was too scary to be true—a pitch-black room in which we were lost forever, unable to find the way out. It worried me just as much, though, to think of the universe having an end. What was on the other side? I pictured a big cement wall floating in outer space, light-years away. At night, I dreamed that I was alone on a spaceship that orbited the earth in gradually widening circles. I didn't know how to turn the ship around or steer it out of its orbit. Outside the window the black sky stretched all around me, and the Earth looked like an old tennis ball, faded and fuzzy. Unable to go back home or to land on another planet, I circled around endlessly.

Now, thirty years later, I think of that dream when I fly to Japan from the American Midwest. On the twelve-hour flight between Detroit and Tokyo or Osaka, I imagine myself traveling in outer space for eternity, always getting farther and farther away from home.

Japan has not been my home for a long time. Though I was born in Kobe, I have not lived there as an adult. I left at twenty to go to college in Illinois, knowing that I would never return. I now live in Green Bay, Wisconsin. I am an American citizen. My life can be divided right down the middle: the first twenty years in Japan, the last twenty years in the American Midwest. I'm not sure if I consider Green Bay to be my "home," exactly. Having grown up in a big city, I am more comfortable in Chicago or Milwaukee. But even the small towns in the Midwest are more like my home than Japan, a country I know only from a child's perspective. I don't understand Japan the way I have come to understand the Midwest—a place I learned gradually as an adult so that I can't remember when I didn't know the things I know now and take for granted. I recall Japan with the bold colors and truncated shapes of a child's perception. My memory seems vivid and yet unreliable.

Since I left, I have made only five short trips to Japan, all of them in the last seven years, all for business, not pleasure. Japan is a country where I was unhappy: my mother killed herself when I was twelve, leaving me to spend my teenage years with my father and stepmother. I usually think of those years as a distant bad memory, but a trip to Japan is like a sudden trip back in time. The minute I board the plane, I become afraid: the past is a black hole waiting to suck me up. When I was in kindergarten, I worried at night that my room was full of invisible holes. If I got out of my bed and started walking, I might fall into one of the holes and be dragged through a big black space; eventually, I would come out into the wrong century or on another planet where no one would know me. I feel the same anxiety as I sit on the plane to Japan, my elbows and knees cramped against the narrow seat: one wrong move and I will be sucked back into the past.

As soon as everyone is seated on the plane, the Japanese announcement welcoming us to the flight reminds me of the polite language I was taught as a child: always speak as though everything in the world were your fault. The bilingual announcements on the plane take twice as long in Japanese as in English because every Japanese announcement begins with a lengthy apology: "We apologize about how long it's taken to seat everyone and thank you for being so patient," "We are so sorry that this has been such a long flight and we very much appreciate the fact that you have been so very cooperative with us," "We apologize for the inconvenience you will no doubt experience in having to fill out the forms we are about to hand out."

Every fourth or fifth sentence has the words *sumimasenga* (I am sorry but) or *osoremasuga* (I fear offending you but) or *yoroshikereba* (if it's all right with you). In the crowded cabin, the polite apologies float toward us like a pleasant mist or gentle spring rain. But actually this politeness is a steel net hauling us into the country where nothing means what it says. Already, before the plane has left American airspace, I have landed in a galaxy of the past, where I can never say what I feel or ask what I want to know.

In my family, proper language has always been an obstacle to understanding. When my brother called me from Japan in

1993, after our father's death, and asked me to come to Japan for a week, he never said or hinted at what he wanted me to do once I got there. I could not arrive in time for the funeral even if I were to leave within the hour. He didn't tell me whether he wanted me to come all the same to show moral support or to discuss financial arrangements. In a businesslike manner, he said, "I was wondering if you could spare a week to come here. I know you're busy with school, but maybe you could make the time if it's not too inconvenient." When I agreed, he added, "It'll be good to see you," as if I were coming to visit him for fun. And I replied, "I'll call my travel agent right away and then call you back," businesslike myself, asking no questions, because we were speaking in Japanese and I didn't know how to ask him what he really wanted.

Our conversation wasn't unusual at all. In Japanese, it's rude to tell people exactly what you need or to ask them what they want. The listener is supposed to guess what the speaker wants from almost nonexistent hints. Someone could talk about the cold weather when she actually wants you to help her pick up some groceries at the store. She won't make an obvious connection between the long talk about the cold weather and the one sentence she might say about going to the store later in the afternoon, the way an English speaker would. A Japanese speaker won't mention these two things in the same conversation. Her talk about the cold weather would not be full of complaints—she might even emphasize how the cold weather is wonderful for her brother, who likes to ski. She won't tell you how she hates the winter or how slippery and dangerous the sidewalks are. But if you don't offer her a ride, you have failed her. My Japanese friends often complain about people who didn't offer to help them at the right time. "But how could these people have known what to do?" I ask. "You didn't tell them." My friends insist, "They should have done it without being asked. It's no good if I have to spell things out to them. They should have been more sensitive."

Having a conversation in Japanese is like driving in the dark without a headlight: every moment, I am on the verge of hitting something and hurting myself or someone else, but I have no way of guessing where the dangers are. Listening to people speak to me in Japanese, over the phone or face to face, I try to figure out what they really mean. I know it's different from what they say, but I have no idea what it is. In my frustration, I turn to the familiar: I begin to analyze the conversation by the Midwestern standard of politeness. Sometimes the comparison helps me because Midwesterners are almost as polite and indirect as Japanese people.

Just like Japanese people, Midwesterners don't like to say no. When they are asked to do something they don't want to do, my Midwestern friends answer, "I'll think about it," or "I'll try." When people say these things in Japanese, everyone knows the real meaning is no. When people in Wisconsin say that they will "think about" attending a party or "try to" be there, there is a good chance that they will actually show up. "I'll think about it" or "I'll try" means that they have not absolutely committed themselves, so if they don't come, people should not be offended. In Japan or in the Midwest, when people don't say yes, I know I should back off and offer, "Don't worry if you can't. It isn't important."

In both cultures, the taboo against saying no applies to anything negative. Once, in Japan, I was speaking with my aunt, Akiko, and my brother. My aunt was about to criticize my stepmother, whom she disliked. Because she was with my brother, who feels differently, Akiko began her conversation by saying, "Now, I know, of course, that your stepmother is a very good person in her own way. She means well and she is so generous."

I could tell that my aunt didn't mean a word of what she said because my Midwestern friends do the exact same thing. They, too, say, "I like So-and-so. We get along just fine, but" before mentioning anything negative about almost anyone. They might then tell a long story about how that person is arrogant, manipulative, or even dishonest, only to conclude the way they started out: "Of course, he is basically a nice person, and we get along fine." They'll nod slightly, as if to say, "We all understand each other." And we do. "I like So-and-so" is simply a disclaimer meant to soften the tone. I expect to hear some version of the disclaimer; I notice when it is omitted. If a friend does not say "So-and-So is a nice person" before and after her long, angry story, I know that she truly dislikes the person she is talking about—so much that the only disclaimer she can make is "I don't like to be so negative, but," making a reference to herself but not to the other person. The omission implies that, as far as she is concerned, the other person no longer deserves her courtesy.

When I go to Japan and encounter the code of Never Say No and Always Use a Disclaimer, I understand what is really meant, because I have come to understand the same things in the Midwest. But sometimes, the similarities between the two forms of politeness are deceptive.

Shortly after my father's death, my uncle, Kenichi—my mother's brother—wanted to pay respects to my father's spirit at the Buddhist altar. I accompanied him and his wife, Mariko, to my stepmother's house, where the altar was kept. Michiko served us lunch and tried to give Kenichi my father's old clothing. She embarrassed me by bragging about the food she was serving and the clothes she was trying to give away, laughing and chattering in her thin, false voice.

As we were getting ready to leave, Michiko invited Kenichi and Mariko to visit her again. She asked them to write down their address and phone number. Squinting at the address Mariko was writing down, my stepmother said, "Hirohata-cho. Is that near the Itami train station?"

"Yes," Mariko replied. "About ten minutes north, on foot." Then, smiling and bowing slightly, she said, "Please come and visit us. I am home every afternoon, except on Wednesdays. If you would call me from the station, I would be very happy to come and meet you there."

"You are welcome to visit here any time, too," Michiko returned, beaming. "You already know where I live, but here is my address anyway." She wrote it down and handed it to Mariko.

Putting the piece of paper in her purse, Mariko bowed and said, "I will look forward to seeing you."

As I walked away from the house with Mariko and Kenichi, I couldn't get over how my stepmother had wangled an invitation out of them. The thought of her coming to their house made me sick, so I asked point-blank, "Are you really going to have Michiko over to your house?"

They looked surprised. Kenichi said, "We didn't mean to

be insincere, but we don't really expect her to come to our house."

"So you were just being polite?" I asked.

"Of course," Kenichi replied.

I would never have guessed the mere formality of their invitation even though polite-but-not-really-meant invitations are nothing new to me. People in Wisconsin often say, "We should get together sometime," or "You should come and have dinner with us soon." When I hear these remarks, I always know which are meant and which are not. When people really mean their invitations, they give a lot of details—where their house is, what is a good time for a visit, how we can get in touch with each other—precisely the kind of details Mariko was giving Michiko. When the invitations are merely polite gestures, they remain timeless and vague. The empty invitations annoy me, especially when they are repeated. They are meant to express good will, but it's silly to keep talking about dinners we will never have. Still, the symbolic invitations in the Midwest don't confuse me; I can always tell them apart from the real thing.

In Japan, there are no clear-cut signs to tell me which invitations are real and which are not. People can give all kinds of details and still not expect me to show up at their door or call them from the train station. I cannot tell when I am about to make a fool of myself or hurt someone's feelings by taking them at their word or by failing to do so.

I don't like to go to Japan because I find it exhausting to speak Japanese all day, every day. What I am afraid of is the language, not the place. Even in Green Bay, when someone insists on speaking to me in Japanese, I clam up after a few words of general greetings, unable to go on.

I can only fall silent because thirty seconds into the conversation, I have already failed at an important task: while I was bowing and saying hello, I was supposed to have been calculating the other person's age, rank, and position in order to determine how polite I should be for the rest of the conversation. In Japanese conversations, the two speakers are almost never on an equal footing: one is senior to the other in age, experience, or rank. Various levels of politeness and formality are required according to these differences: it is rude to be too familiar, but people are equally offended if you are too formal, sounding snobbish and untrusting. Gender is as important as rank. Men and women practically speak different languages; women's language is much more indirect and formal than men's. There are words and phrases that women are never supposed to say, even though they are not crude or obscene. Only a man can say *damare* (shut up). No matter how angry she is, a woman must say, *shizukani* (quiet).

Until you can find the correct level of politeness, you can't go on with the conversation: you won't even be able to address the other person properly. There are so many Japanese words for the pronoun *you. Anata* is a polite but intimate *you* a woman would use to address her husband, lover, or a very close woman friend, while a man would say *kimi*, which is informal, or *omae*, which is so informal that a man would say this word only to a family member; *otaku* is informal but impersonal, so it should be used with friends rather than family. Though there are these various forms of *you*, most people address each other in the third person—it is offensive to call someone *you* directly. To a woman named Hanako Maeda, you don't say, "Would you like to go out for lunch?" You say, "Would Maeda-san (Miss Maeda) like to go out for lunch?" But if you had known Hanako for a while, maybe you should call her Hanako-san instead of Maeda-san, especially if you are also a woman and not too much younger than she. Otherwise, she might think that you are too formal and unfriendly. The word for lunch also varies: *hirumeshi* is another casual word only a man is allowed to say, *hirugohan* is informal but polite enough for friends, *ohirugohan* is a little more polite, *chushoku* is formal and businesslike, and *gochushoku* is the most formal and businesslike.

All these rules mean that before you can get on with any conversation beyond the initial greetings, you have to agree on your relationship—which one of you is superior, how close you expect to be, who makes the decisions and who defers. So why even talk, I always wonder. The conversation that follows the mutual sizing-up can only be an empty ritual, a careful enactment of our differences rather than a chance to get to know each other or to exchange ideas.

Talking seems especially futile when I have to address a man in Japanese. Every word I say forces me to be elaborately polite, indirect, submissive, and unassertive. There is no way I can sound intelligent, clearheaded, or decisive. But if I did not speak a "proper" feminine language, I would sound stupid in another way—like someone who is uneducated, insensitive, and rude, and therefore cannot be taken seriously. I never speak Japanese with the Japanese man who teaches physics at the college where I teach English. We are colleagues, meant to be equals. The language I use should not automatically define me as second best.

Meeting Japanese-speaking people in the States makes me nervous for another reason. I have nothing in common with these people except that we speak Japanese. Our meeting seems random and artificial, and I can't get over the oddness of addressing a total stranger in Japanese. In the twenty years I lived in Japan, I rarely had a conversation with someone I didn't already know. The only exception was the first day of school in seventh grade, when none of us knew one another, or when I was introduced to my friends' parents. Talking to clerks at stores scarcely counts. I never chatted with people I was doing business with. This is not to say that I led a particularly sheltered life. My experience was typical of anyone—male or female—growing up in Japan.

In Japan, whether you are a child or an adult, ninety-five percent of the people you talk to are your family, relatives, old friends, neighbors, and people you work or go to school with every day. The only new people you meet are connected to these people you already know—friends of friends, new spouses of your relatives—and you are introduced to them formally. You don't all of a sudden meet someone new. My friends and I were taught that no "nice" girl would talk to strangers on trains or at public places. It was bad manners to gab with shopkeepers or with repair people, being too familiar and keeping them from work. While American children are cautioned not to speak with strangers for reasons of safety, we were taught not to do so because it wasn't "nice." Even the most rebellious of us obeyed. We had no language in which we could address a stranger even if we had wanted to.

Traveling in Japan or simply taking the commuter train in Kobe now, I notice the silence around me. It seems oppressive that you cannot talk to someone who is looking at your favorite painting at a museum or sitting next to you on the train, reading a book that you finished only last week. In Japan, you can't even stop strangers and ask for simple directions when you are lost. If you get lost, you look for a policeman, who will help you because that is part of his job.

A Japanese friend and I got lost in Yokohama one night after we came out of a restaurant. We were looking for the train station and had no idea where it was, but my friend said, "Well, we must be heading in the right direction, since most people seem to be walking that way. It's late now. They must be going back to the station, too." After about ten minutes—with no train station in sight yet—my friend said that if she had been lost in New York or Paris, she would have asked one of the people we were following. But in her own country, in her own language, it was unthinkable to approach a stranger.

For her, asking was not an option. That's different from when people in the Midwest choose not to stop at a gas station for directions or flag down a store clerk to locate some item on the shelves. Midwestern people don't like to ask because they don't want to call attention to themselves by appearing stupid and helpless. Refusing to ask is a matter of pride and self-reliance—a matter of choice. Even the people who pride themselves on never asking know that help is readily available. In Japan, approaching a stranger means breaking an unspoken rule of public conduct.

The Japanese code of silence in public places does offer a

certain kind of protection. In Japan, everyone is shielded from unwanted intrusion or attention, and that isn't entirely bad. In public places in the States, we all wish, from time to time, that people would go about their business in silence and leave us alone. Just the other day in the weight room of the YMCA, a young man I had never met before told me that he had been working out for the last two months and gained fifteen pounds. "I've always been too thin," he explained. "I want to gain twenty more pounds, and I'm going to put it all up here." We were sitting side by side on different machines. He indicated his shoulders and chest by patting them with his hand. "That's nice," I said, noncommittal but polite. "Of course," he continued, "I couldn't help putting some of the new weight around my waist, too." To my embarrassment, he lifted his shirt and pointed at his stomach. "Listen," I told him. "You don't have to show it to me or anything." I got up from my machine even though I wasn't finished. Still, I felt obligated to say, "Have a nice workout," as I walked away.

I don't appreciate discussing a complete stranger's weight gain and being shown his stomach, and it's true that bizarre conversations like that would never happen in a Japanese gym. Maybe there is comfort in knowing that you will never have to talk to strangers—that you can live your whole life surrounded by friends and family who will understand what you mean without your saying it. Silence can be a sign of harmony among close friends or family, but silent harmony doesn't help people who disagree or don't fit in. On crowded trains in Kobe or Tokyo, where people won't even make eye contact with strangers, much less talk to them, I feel as though each one of us were sealed inside an invisible capsule, unable to breathe or speak out. It is just like my old dream of being stuck inside a spaceship orbiting the earth. I am alarmed by how lonely I feel—and by how quietly content everyone else seems to be.

In Japanese, I don't have a voice for speaking my mind. When a Japanese flight attendant walks down the aisle in her traditional kimono, repeating the endlessly apologetic announcements in the high, squeaky voice a nice woman is expected to use in public, my heart sinks because hers is the voice I am supposed to mimic. All my childhood friends answer their telephones in this same voice, as do the young women store clerks welcoming people and thanking them for their business or TV anchor women reading the news. It doesn't matter who we are or what we are saying. A woman's voice is always the same: a childish squeak piped from the throat.

The first time I heard that voice coming out of my own mouth, about three years ago, I was lost at a subway station in Osaka. Though there were plenty of people gathered around the wall map I was trying to read, I did not stop any of them. I flagged down a station attendant, identifiable by his blue uniform. *"Ano, sumimasen,"* I started immediately with an apology ("Well, I'm so sorry to be bothering you"). Then I asked where I could catch the right train. Halfway through my inquiry, I realized that I was squeezing the air through my tightly constricted throat, making my voice thin and wavering. *I have to get out of here,* I thought. *It's a good thing I'm leaving in just a few days.*

I was afraid of being stuck in Japan, unable to speak except in that little-bird voice. I'm afraid of the same thing every time I go there.

People often tell me that I am lucky to be bilingual, but I am not so sure. Language is like a radio. I have to choose a specific station, English or Japanese, and tune in. I can't listen to both at the same time. In between, there is nothing but static. These days, though, I find myself listening to static because I am afraid to turn my dial to the Japanese station and hear that bird-woman voice. Trying to speak Japanese in Japan, I'm still thinking in English. I can't turn off what I really want to say and concentrate on what is appropriate. Flustered, I try to work out a quick translation, but my feelings are untranslatable and my voice is the voice of a foreigner. The whole experience reminds me of studying French in college and being unable to say or write what I thought.

In my second-year French class, I had to keep a journal. I could only say stupid things: "I got up at six. I ate breakfast. It's cold. I'm tired." I was reduced to making these idiotic statements because I didn't have the language to explain, "It's cold for September and I feel sad that summer is over. But I try to cheer myself up by thinking of how beautiful the trees will be in a month." In my French, it was either cold or not cold. Nothing in between, no discussion of what the weather meant. After finishing my entry every day, I felt depressed: my life sounded bleak when it was reduced to bad weather and meal schedules, but I wasn't fluent enough in French to talk about anything else. Now, my Japanese feels thin in the same way.

In any language, it is hard to talk about feelings, and there are things that are almost unsayable because they sound too harsh, painful, or intimate. When we are fluent, though, we can weave and dodge our way through the obstacles and get to the difficult thing we want to say; each of us weaves and dodges in slightly different ways, using our individual style or voice. In the way we say the almost unsayable, we can hear the subtle modulations and shifts that make each of our voices unique.

When I studied the poetry of Maxine Kumin, Anne Sexton, and Sylvia Plath in college, I was immediately drawn to their voices. I still love the eloquence with which these poets talk about daily life and declare their feelings, balancing gracefully between matter-of-fact observations and powerful emotions. After a particularly emotional statement, the poets often step back and resume describing the garden, the yew trees and blackberries, before returning to the feelings again. They say the almost unsayable by balancing on the edge of saying too much and then pulling back, only to push their way toward that edge again. Reading them in college, I wanted to learn to speak with a voice like theirs.

My whole schooling has been a process of acquiring a voice. In college and graduate school, I learned to speak, write, and think like my favorite writers—through imitation and emulation, the way anyone learns any language. I have not had the same experience in Japanese. The only voice I was taught was the one that squeezed my throat shut every time I wanted to say, *Help me. This is what I want. Let me tell you how I feel.*

On my trips to Japan, I am nervous and awake the whole way. Sitting stiffly upright in the cone of orange light, I read my favorite novelists in English: Margaret Atwood, Amy Tan,

Anne Tyler. I cannot shed my fear of the Japanese language. When the plane begins its descent toward Tokyo or Osaka and the final sets of announcements are made in the two languages, I don't try to switch from the English station of my mind to the Japanese. I turn the dial a little closer to the Japanese station without turning off the English, even though my mind will fill with static and the Japanese I speak will be awkward and inarticulate. I am willing to compromise my proficiency in Japanese so that I can continue to think the thoughts I have come to value in English.

Yet as the plane tips to the right and then to the left, I feel the pull of the ground. Gravity and nostalgia seem one and the same. Poised over the land of my childhood, I recognize the coastline. The sea shines and glitters just like the one in the old songs we sang in grade school. The mountains are a dark green and densely textured. It comes to me, like a surprise, that I love this scenery. *How could I have spent my adult life away from here?* I wonder. *This is where I should have been all along.* I remember the low, gray hills of the Midwest and wonder how I could have found them beautiful, when I grew up surrounded by real mountains. But even as part of me feels nostalgic, another part of me remains guarded, and my adult voice talks in the back of my mind like a twenty-four-hour broadcast. *Remember who you were,* it warns, *but don't forget who you are now.*

CHAPTER TWO

FAMILY

❊

When people ask me about my brother, I find myself mumbling a polite but lame disclaimer: "Jumpei is a very nice person and I like him. We get along just fine, but . . ."

What follows is not criticism but something possibly worse.

"But I don't really know him," I have to admit. "He's like a nice guy I scarcely know."

Jumpei is my only immediate family left, but I have seen him only four times in the last twenty years. He spends the year traveling in South America, buying sweaters, rugs, and jewelry to sell in Japan. He doesn't stay anywhere long enough to receive letters. Most of the time, I don't know where he is.

As children, we never imagined that we would live our adult lives in foreign countries, so far away from each other. My brother and I grew up in a series of small suburban houses, our rooms always right next to each other's. Before our mother's death, the three of us were like a single-parent family during the week, though on weekends and during summers, we belonged to a large extended family. We hardly saw our father, Hiroshi, who left for work before we got up, came home after we were asleep, and took numerous out-of-town business trips. This work schedule was typical of men his age, but Hiroshi was also gone on weekends—playing rugby or golf with his old college friends—while other people's fathers fixed things around the house, took their children to the zoo, or sat in the living room watching TV. Jumpei and I spent our weekends going on picnics, swimming at the beach, or hiking in the mountains with our mother, Takako. We visited our grandparents, uncles, aunts, and cousins on her side, and also our father's sister, Akiko, and her daughter Kazumi. If we had been asked to name our family in grade school, we would have named each other, our mother, and then added, "and our father, who's never home," before moving on to a long list of relations. We knew we were family to each other, then.

Though Jumpei was taught to call me "Oneichan" (big sister) as a form of respect, I wasn't a very good sister. When my brother and his friends wanted to play with my friends and me, I talked my group into running to a hiding place. "Leave us alone. Go play by yourselves," we yelled before dashing away, leaving the younger kids to cry. Like most brothers and sisters, though, we would have gotten closer as we grew older. But our mother's death changed everything.

The afternoon our mother decided to end her life, my brother and I were shopping downtown with Hiroshi. It was one of the few Sundays our father ever spent with us. We came home to find Takako unconscious on the floor with the windows shut and the gas pipe held to her mouth. Hiroshi turned off the gas, laid out the futon in his room, carried her there, and called a friend of his, a surgeon. His friend agreed to drive to our house to try to resuscitate Takako. Hiroshi told him that he would run out to the main road down the hill and meet him there so that he would not get lost.

By the time Hiroshi was off the phone and opening the windows, my brother and I were sitting down on the tatami floor next to the futon, looking down at our mother. Jumpei was crying. I was not. Because I had known how unhappy our mother was, I wasn't surprised. I had the feeling that my worst nightmare had come true—I was scared and my heart was beating very fast, but everything seemed familiar, as if I should have predicted it. Hiroshi came and sat down next to me so that I was between him and Jumpei, all of us looking at Takako with our heads bent down.

"It'll be all right," Hiroshi mumbled, more to me than to Jumpei. "Don't worry."

I turned to him then, and the two of us stared at each other, listening to my brother cry. We did not embrace each other or cry. We did not touch my brother on the shoulder or pat his head to comfort him. More than likely, it was already too late for the two of us to give or offer comfort. I was a sister who ran away with her friends while her younger brother cried. My father, as I would find out later, was already having an affair with Michiko, the woman he would start living with only a month later and marry within a year. The only person who held the three of us together and made us feel like family was my mother, who was dying by her own choice.

All these years later, I keep picturing my father, brother,

and me sitting together in that small room for a few minutes before Hiroshi went away to meet the doctor. Even though I lived with Hiroshi and Jumpei for eight more years, I think of those few minutes as the last time the three of us were together. It was the last time all of us were feeling the same things: panic, remorse, and an urge, however vague, to stick together, to turn to one another for comfort. When Hiroshi said, "It'll be all right. Don't worry," he must have meant to say more, to offer stronger assurances. I'm sorry that neither of us could keep the conversation going. I wish we had cried or embraced and said something. If that was not the last moment we were a family, then certainly it was the last moment we could have become one.

Jumpei and I went to live with our aunt, Akiko, for a month before returning to our father's house, where Michiko had moved in. For the next eight years when both of us lived at home, our bedrooms were next to each other's, separated only by a narrow hallway. We never crossed this hallway to go into each other's room. Every night, I was in my room studying or reading and seldom came out. I could hear my brother laughing and chatting with Michiko downstairs in the kitchen, spending the whole evening there. Hiroshi still worked late, but he was home on Sundays now, watching TV with Michiko all day. Both he and Jumpei loved to be with Michiko—one of them was always in the kitchen or the living room, laughing with her. But it was never the three of them. They were both close to Michiko, but not to each other, and I was close to nobody. Alone in my upstairs bedroom, I imagined myself on a hot-air balloon, drifting away.

After I left home, I did not see my brother again for

twelve years. Finally, while I was living in Green Bay with my husband, Chuck, Jumpei visited us, bringing an American friend. It wasn't much of a visit, really. Jumpei said they were on the way to a camping trip and could stay only one night. In the morning, before they left, we all went to a restaurant for breakfast.

"My mother would love to have a sports car like yours," Jumpei said to Chuck and me while we waited for our food. "My mother loves to drive. She drives rather aggressively, like a man." He chuckled in the amused way people do when they are talking about someone they love.

A little later, I said something about "our stepmother."

Jumpei's friend, Jeff, looked surprised. He said to my brother, "Oh, I didn't know that your parents were divorced. Your father is remarried and you have a stepmother?"

"No," I said. "I mean, yes, but not in the way you think. Our father is remarried and we both have a stepmother, but that's because our real mother is dead. The woman Jumpei calls 'my mother' is actually our stepmother."

I looked across the table at Jumpei, who turned away and would not look back at me. He stammered a little and announced to the whole table, "Well, that's true. But she is my mother, really. At least, she's the only mother I remember."

That's how I found out that Jumpei remembers almost nothing about Takako. At first, I couldn't believe that. I have a lot of memories of Takako from before I was eight. If I could remember going to the zoo with her at five, how could he forget about our summer trip to the seaside when he was seven or the weekends Takako took us to the pool after we were both in grade school? When our mother kept crickets in glass jars, Jumpei cut up the watermelon and eggplant to feed them every day and spent hours listening to them sing; he was the one who cried in October when one by one, the crickets died—to comfort him, our mother told us stories about crickets going to insect heaven where they flew around all day eating big watermelon slices. How could he forget her stories?

But there was one big difference between Jumpei and me. Our mother had been there until I was twelve to help me remember: when I was nine, ten, and eleven she and I would reminisce together, "Remember when you were in kindergarten and we went to see the fireflies by the river?" "Remember our old house and that dog who lived across the street?" By the time I was twelve, I remembered these long-ago events as though they were old stories I had memorized. The reminiscences we shared were the stories of my life, of my mother's and my life together. My brother didn't have the same chance. By the time he was twelve, there was no one to tell him the stories of his life.

I could have been—should have been—that person. Instead of staying shut up in my room, studying and feeling sorry for myself, I should have spent my teenage years taking care of my brother. That's what I had been taught to do, what I had promised my mother. When I called her from downtown on what turned out to be the afternoon of her suicide, my mother said, "You are a nice girl, Kyoko—a considerate person. Be good and take care of your brother for me." That was the last thing she said to me; as soon as we got home, I knew that she had meant it for a lifetime, not just for that afternoon.

I didn't keep that promise, even though I had been trained all my life to do just that. When I was in kindergarten and my brother was a baby learning to crawl, my family lived in a two-story house with a steep stairway. My mother asked one of her brothers to come and put in a wooden gate at the top of the staircase to keep Jumpei from tumbling down. It was a swinging gate that snapped shut and could be locked. She showed me what I should do every time I came upstairs, where my brother's nursery and my own room were: I should make sure that the gate was locked.

"Pay attention," she said. "I want you to be careful so your brother doesn't get hurt."

She kept shutting and locking the gate, then making me do it on my own until I got it right. When I slid the metal into its proper place, the lock made such a satisfying sound: a little sigh of sliding metal and then the decisive click. My mother was trying to teach me to be careful. She wanted me to know the sound that meant safety.

I can still picture her, a woman younger than I am now, standing on the landing at that house. As she looked down on the steps, she must have imagined her son tumbling down headfirst. For her, love meant worry—she was always imagining us falling down, getting lost, getting hurt. She was constantly thinking of ways to prevent these catastrophes.

Now that my brother and I are the only members of our family, I wish I had worried more about him when we lived together. I should have imagined the worst for him and tried to prevent it, the way our mother wanted me to.

It's years too late. My brother doesn't need me. The last time we saw each other, in Japan, I was staying at my aunt's house, and he was at our stepmother's. We only got together twice, never just by ourselves. We parted after a few days, exchanging polite invitations neither of us would follow up on. He was going back to Tokyo to work, even though I was staying in the country for another week.

After he was gone, I realized that my brother and I do have a few things in common. Neither of us ever felt really related to our father, and his death has left us more puzzled than sad. Hiroshi will always be a mystery to us, a man whose behavior seemed only bizarre and annoying, never loving or fatherly. During our visit, Jumpei and I shared a few bitter laughs over anecdotes about our father's impatience and insensitivity. "Remember when he used to yell at people at train stations for bumping into him or skipping in front of him in the ticket lines?" Jumpei asked me. "I always walked a few steps away and looked the other way, hoping that no one would think I was with him." I had similar stories, too. But Jumpei and I could only talk about our father with sarcasm, emphasizing what an odd person he was—we never told each other how hurt we used to feel by his indifference, how scared we were of his bad temper. Unable to mention our feelings, we talked on as if the whole thing was a joke, each of us trying to sound ironic and detached.

Jumpei and I don't have a real home country, just as we didn't have a "real" father. But our talk about feeling homeless is always ironic and cheerful. When Jumpei says he feels more comfortable in Colombia or Ecuador than he does in Japan, he doesn't show any regret; he dreams of settling in South America someday, visiting Japan for only a week every year to take care of his wholesale business and to say hello to his "mother." We laugh, exchanging stories about how relieved we are the moment the plane leaves Tokyo or Osaka for overseas. "The rat race of Japan," we say to each other, "it gives me the creeps." I have never told him that I some-times envy people who seem perfectly content to belong where they were born, or about the pitiful tone I try to keep out of my voice when I have to tell people, "I don't really have a family." If Jumpei feels similar regret or sadness, I will never know it. My brother and I can talk only about what we don't have—father, country, a close family—and laugh with calculated detachment. We never mention the feelings we might share and console each other about.

In Milwaukee, I used to live near a church that had a sculpture on the front lawn. The sculpture was made of two identical concrete blocks, each with a notch in the middle, placed about a foot apart on the grass. The arrangement looked abstract and industrial. I never could understand the significance of the sculpture until a friend pointed out that the negative space between the two blocks formed a cross. My brother and I are like the two parts of that sculpture. Whatever we share is in the negative space between us. We mirror each other from a distance; we can never touch or connect.

A few of my friends in Wisconsin are very close to their brothers or sisters. I saw one of them, Mary, at a party last March. It was a dreary evening with gray snow coming down. Everyone was depressed by the weather.

"I turned forty last weekend," Mary said. "I'm divorced, the weather's terrible, and I just broke up with the man I was seeing for two years."

Mary was there with her sister, who looks so much like her that they are often mistaken for twins.

"My sister's taking care of me," Mary continued. "I didn't even want to come here tonight, but she dragged me out. She tells me that it's good to get out. She doesn't want me to sit around feeling depressed. She's been bringing me food every day."

While Mary was talking to me, her sister was getting coffee for the two of them. Watching her walk across the floor toward us, two cups and saucers balanced in her hands, I felt completely envious. All their lives, they will be sisters. Divorces and break-ups and bad weather don't mean the same thing if you can count on family.

Mary is a lucky exception. Most people don't feel as close to their siblings as they wish they did. Like me, they'll say, "My brother (or sister) is a very nice person, but we don't really understand each other. We have very little in common."

My friend Jim, a photographer, has a younger brother who is a businessman. When Jim told him that he was going to Nevada to take landscape photographs, his brother said, "Why are you going there? There's nothing out there."

"How do you know?" Jim asked him. "Have you ever been to Nevada?"

"No," his brother said, "but I've flown over it many times. Believe me. I know. There's nothing out there."

Though Jim laughed about the conversation, I think he was saddened a little, too, by how different he and his brother had grown up to be. What was most important to Jim—his photography, the beauty of almost empty spaces—didn't mean anything to his brother.

When I feel sad about not having a family, I tell myself that all kinds of people feel disconnected from their families.

The only thing that makes my brother and me different is that we scarcely share a past. While my friends recall growing up in the same family with their siblings and wonder how they turned out to be so different, my brother and I don't recall the same people as our family: he has his mother, I have mine.

Some of my relatives feel more like immediate family to me than my brother does. My cousin, Kazumi, and I have always been close. On our last visit, while we were having tea in her sitting room, I noticed a boat-shaped vase in which she had arranged five roses. Each rose was fully open—the pale gold of the outer petals gradually darkening toward the salmon-pink center. "What color are these roses?" I asked. "The color is called champagne. It's a new hybrid," Kazumi said. The flowers reminded me of the dresses of the dolls we played with as children.

When Kazumi and I were two or three, someone gave us identical dolls, larger than we were. My doll, Emi, had a red dress and Kazumi's doll, Eri, had a pink dress. For years, I brought my doll to her house when my mother, brother, and I visited Akiko and Kazumi. While our mothers drank tea in the kitchen and Jumpei played on the floor at their feet, Kazumi and I went to her room upstairs, carrying the dolls. We set them down side by side against the wall, carefully smoothing out their long hair and ruffled dresses. When the dolls were properly seated, Kazumi would place her ceramic tea set in front of them. It was an old but real set her mother had given her. Because Kazumi was careful and gentle, she could play with a real ceramic tea set. If the same set had been given to me, I would have broken every single cup in a week and cried about it, trying to blame someone else for my own carelessness.

While the dolls were having tea, Kazumi and I sat at her desk, cutting out photographs of people, furniture, and food from the women's magazines Aunt Akiko subscribed to. We kept the pictures in flat, square cardboard boxes, which we pretended were apartment complexes. We had to make sure that each box had the right number of people and enough furniture and food. When any box became too crowded, we had to start a new one. I would never have played this paper-families game with anyone else, so patiently cutting out the photographs without amputating people's legs or arms or decapitating them, on purpose or by accident.

Kazumi was the only girl I knew who wanted to play like a girl. My other close friends were boys who lived in the neighborhood or girls who wanted to play dodgeball and catch grasshoppers. On the rare occasions these girls and I played with dolls, we snapped off the arms and legs and traded them so each doll looked ridiculous with someone else's leg or arm. Posing the dolls so they looked like a group of mutants, my friends and I would cackle, pretending to be queens of freaks and witches.

Kazumi was entirely different. She wanted our two dolls to have tea and enjoy a nice quiet visit—the kind of visit our mothers wanted us to have together—while we cut out paper families, making sure that every household was comfortably provided for. Kazumi and I would never have been friends if we hadn't been cousins: we were too different to have chosen each other. But that's precisely what family is—a connection that links Jim and his brother even if one travels hundreds of miles to photograph the landscape the other dismisses as "nothing." What makes us family has nothing to do with similar interests, compatibility, or choice. Kazumi and I have come to love each other out of habit, out of our long association. I worry about her, as my mother used to worry about my brother and me. Now that her mother is gone, I imagine her living alone with her flowers and I worry about her loneliness; I wake up some nights dreaming about her and think, "What if she got sick? What if there was another earthquake in Kobe and her house was damaged?" I wish that I could be there to grow old with her as old friends and family are meant to.

What I miss most from not having family close by is a sense that the past is an open and growing manuscript, expansive and forgiving. When we talk about the past with family, we often find that each of us remembers different aspects of the same experience. Though the difference in memory can sometimes lead to bickering, it's a relief to know that none of us has the sole responsibility for remembering—what we forget will be recalled by someone else. We occasionally learn details we didn't know because we were too young at the time or lived too far away. Family stories can shed a new light on the events we think we know. After the conversation, we add the new pieces to our memory. In this way, the past can expand rather than shrink. I look forward to seeing my mother's family on my short visits to Japan because that's one of the few times I can experience memory expanding.

The last time I saw my uncle, Kenichi, he had just finished reading my first novel, *Shizuko's Daughter*, in the Japanese translation. Many of the details in the novel's setting come from my grandparents' house in the country—the house where Kenichi had grown up. He was glad that I had included the child's wooden slide my grandfather built when my mother was born, the purple lantern flowers my grandmother used to grow, the cicadas that were always buzzing in the trees in the yard.

"I was amazed by how much you could remember," he said.

"Of course I remember a lot," I reassured him. His own kids, fifteen years younger than I, do not recall our grandparents in the same way—they were just babies when our grandfather died; by the time they were growing up, our grandmother was in her eighties and no longer able to take long walks with them or grow as many flowers in her garden as she used to. Kenichi was happy to have me remember and write about what his kids could not, so that the memories are kept alive.

"There's one thing I felt really bad about," Kenichi confessed. "I thought about it the whole time I was reading your novel."

"What was that?" I asked him, leaning forward over the table where we were having dinner.

"Remember those diaries your mother kept when she was in high school?" he asked. "There were many of them, in those glossy, yellow notebooks."

"Yes," I said. "I have them." Shortly after I left for college, my grandmother had found them in the attic of her house and sent them to me.

"But you don't have all the volumes," Kenichi said. "Do you know why?"

I shook my head. There were a few months missing here

and there, but I always assumed that one or two notebooks must have gotten misplaced.

"When your mother finished high school and was in Kobe, working as a secretary, I was living in that house in the country with your grandparents and your Aunt Keiko. We were just kids." Kenichi paused.

I nodded, encouraging him to go on. Kenichi is sixteen years younger than my mother, who was the oldest of six children.

"Those diaries were already in the attic then. When I was in grade school, I found them there. The notebooks had such beautiful white paper—thick and glossy. I was only eight or nine, you have to remember. I tore the pages out and made paper airplanes. Every day, I would sit on top of the stairs, tear out page after page of your mother's diary, and fold paper airplanes. I watched them flying down the stairs. I got pretty good at folding planes. Some of them went quite a long way. That's how a couple of those notebooks got lost. When I read your novel, I remembered that and felt so bad." Kenichi made a face. "I can't believe how stupid I was as a kid," he concluded.

"Don't worry about it," I said, feeling suddenly so happy that I was laughing. I was imagining hundreds of white paper airplanes flying. "Your telling me about it now makes up for everything."

I'm not sure if Kenichi was convinced. I couldn't explain my feelings to him very well. But maybe it doesn't matter. In the book of my past, there is now a new image of my uncle as a young boy sitting on the stairway and flying paper airplanes, made of beautiful paper, with my mother's words in their precise creases. Kenichi might think that each plane deprived me of a page of my mother's writing, a page of memory, but the opposite is true. I see those planes floating down the stairway toward me, passed on from Kenichi to me because we share a past and we both loved my mother—because we belong to the same family. I cannot ask for more, except the impossible: that I had the eloquence to tell my uncle, in his language, what I can only write in mine.

CHAPTER THREE

SECRETS

❉

In seventh grade, when a friend sent me a book from the island of Kyushu, I held it in my hand, marveling at the layer of fine white dust on the clear plastic cover. I couldn't believe that I was looking at dust from another island. I didn't know that Kyushu was only a few hours from Kobe by train.

In Japan, it is easy to travel from one city to another on a different island, or from a far suburb to the heart of Tokyo. The route maps and train schedules are posted on the walls of every station, as are the signs indicating the appropriate tracks and fares. Uniformed attendants are on duty to answer questions. No matter where I am going, I can buy a ticket from an automated machine, walk to the designated track, and board the right train. Everything is clear. It's almost impossible to get lost.

And yet, once I get off the train, I can't travel the last few miles or blocks to my destination on my own. I will not be able to locate a particular house or apartment building from the address. Even a cab driver will get lost unless I can point out landmarks only the people in that neighborhood would know—a small tobacco shop on the corner, a bamboo fence around someone's house. In Japanese cities, only a few major thoroughfares have names; the other streets are known as "that street where the Tanaka family lives in the big white house" or "the street that borders the park where you used to play." No outsider would have that kind of information.

Japanese addresses look deceptively simple and logical. I used to live at 12–17 Matsugaoka-cho, Nishinomiya-shi. The address meant that ours was the seventeenth house in the twelfth section of the area (cho) called Matsugaoka in the city of Nishinomiya. But since none of the narrow, winding streets in my cho had names, there was no way to describe where the eleventh section ended and the twelfth began, or why our house was number 17 instead of number 22. Only close friends, neighbors, or relatives who had visited before could find our house. Everyone in the entire Kobe-Osaka area knew how to get to the train station near our house, but even people who lived a mile away in the next cho could not find my house unless I were to meet them at the station and show them the way.

That is the paradox of Japan: the discrepancy between what everyone knows about public places and what almost no one knows about private ones. This isn't only about places or addresses. The difficulty I have finding someone's house in Japan reminds me of the difficulty I have navigating all of Japanese private life.

In Japan, public knowledge is like public transportation: accessible, uniform, and convenient. Even in the remotest,

smallest village on the southern island, you can get a newspaper that reports major world and national events on its
front page rather than whether the high school baseball team
won or lost. What you can't find out, no matter where you
live in the country, concerns your own health, money, or
legal rights. It's the opposite of what I experience in Green
Bay, where I find the same football news repeated two or
three times in the same paper and have to wait an hour for
the bus if my car breaks down. Though I appreciate the better public transportation and information when I travel to
Japan, I ultimately feel diminished: I'm not used to feeling so
helpless about my own private life.

In America, I feel confused by large-scale public issues:
the state of the environment, the various plans to cut taxes or
to decrease government spending, the decline or the improvement of public education, the gap between the rich and
the poor. These issues are as overwhelming as the large public places where I get lost: shopping malls, stadium parking
lots, or highway interchanges, many of which have misleading or badly lit signs. I am irritated by the newspaper or
television equivalents of those bad signs—headlines that
make local and road construction seem more important than
the peace talks in the Middle East, thirty-minute hometown
news shows that update the weather four times even when
conditions are normal. I often wish that I could get better
information, but I don't lose sleep over bad news coverage. I
don't expect to be an expert on every public issue.

My immediate private life is a different matter. I have a
very high standard of knowledge when it comes to my own
life. Even though I may be confused about how my senator
voted on the last health care or tax reduction bill, I expect to

be well informed about my health, bank accounts, debts, or legal rights. No one in America likes to be kept in the dark about his or her health, money, or legal rights and told to trust; very few people choose to remain ignorant. I am no exception.

My Japanese relatives don't share the same eagerness for knowledge, even in life-and-death situations. Both my father and his sister remained ignorant about their cancers until they died. No one told them and they asked no questions. If they sensed that they were dying, they didn't talk about it. Neither did their doctors—at least not to Hiroshi and Akiko themselves.

In Japan, doctors usually inform the immediate family of terminally ill patients and ask them to keep quiet. The patients, the doctors advise, may lose heart and die in a few weeks if they find out the truth. "Don't discourage them and shorten their lives," the doctors warn. "Besides, they should be happy and content in the short time they have left, not worried and afraid." Most families agree. They tell the truth to relatives, old friends, and a few business associates, but always with a warning: "Of course, he/she doesn't know, so don't let on."

My American friend Vince, who teaches in Japan, once told me about a friend who had cancer but didn't know about it until he finished his two-year appointment at a Japanese college and went back to the States. His friend had consulted a Japanese doctor about his stomach pains and had had some tests done. In retrospect, Vince's friend was sure that his Japanese doctor had known about his cancer from these tests but had never told him.

Hearing this story, I felt angry. If I were dying, I thought,

I would want to be the first to know the truth. I should be the one to tell my family and friends. In Japan, the whole order is reversed: doctors make decisions for you without your knowledge, and families tiptoe around an obvious truth, everyone wrapped in polite silence. The assumption behind it—that people don't know what is best for themselves—scares me.

Vince and I had this discussion the same year Hiroshi and Akiko became ill. Akiko had surgery because something was wrong with her liver. Neither she nor her daughter Kazumi mentioned cancer. Hiroshi, too, was hospitalized for nine weeks. He and my stepmother told me that he had had surgery to remove benign polyps from his intestines.

I suspect now that both my father and my aunt already had cancer back then and had surgery to remove the tumors. But because I was talking to them in Japan, in Japanese, it didn't occur to me to try to know more than I was told. I never made the connection between Vince's story and my family's illness. Maybe that's the real danger of speaking and thinking in a constant cloud of polite vague language: the language numbs my thinking. I stop raising questions, even to myself. When my brother called in April 1993 to say that our father had died from cancer, I was completely surprised.

As it turned out, my father recovered well from his initial surgery and was back to his normal health for about a year and a half. Then his cancer returned and he had several operations to remove more tumors. In October 1992, after one of these operations, the doctor finally told my stepmother that my father had cancer, that the tumors were too widespread for additional surgery or treatment. The doctor predicted that Hiroshi could still live for a year—and told Michiko to say nothing to him. My stepmother told Akiko and a few of Hiroshi's business friends; when my brother returned from South America, she told him, too. Akiko wanted Michiko to telephone me, but Michiko decided against telling me anything. While Akiko was trying to find ways to notify me—without directly going against Michiko's wishes—my father died.

I resent Michiko for not having told me. But at least I understand why she kept a secret from me. Michiko never liked me. She was happy that my brother and I were on distant and even hostile terms with Hiroshi. She often reminded us about how the three of us never got along. She loved to tell stories about the things I said when I was thirteen or fourteen—how I told my father that if I'd had a choice, I would rather not have been born than be born his daughter. It's no surprise that she didn't want me to know that my father was dying. She was afraid that I might decide to visit him and that we might come to some understanding. If I knew the truth, maybe I would try to make peace. After years of making our already bad relationship worse, she didn't want a last-minute reconciliation between us.

Michiko's secrecy was hostile and malicious. That kind of secrecy is not unusual; withholding information is the way a lot of people hurt and manipulate others. Michiko's behavior angers me but there is nothing puzzling about it. What I can't understand is the polite secret everyone—not only Michiko but also Akiko and my brother—kept from Hiroshi while he was dying. They said nothing because they didn't want to scare or hurt him. Their intention was the opposite of malice.

Michiko, Akiko, Jumpei, and the doctors weren't the only

people keeping secrets. Hiroshi himself must have known that he was seriously ill, that he was dying, that the numerous operations he'd had were to remove malignant tumors. In Japan, doctors keep patients in hospitals for several weeks after even minor surgery. Hiroshi convalesced for nine weeks after the removal of his supposedly benign polyps. And yet he was sent home a few weeks after his last surgery, and the doctors didn't recommend any more treatment. Being sent home so easily is a sign that you are not expected to recover. Hiroshi must have realized the seriousness of his illness, but he never asked his doctors or his family to tell him more. Perhaps he was afraid. Or else he did not want to put Michiko, Jumpei, or Akiko in the awkward position of having to lie to him. My father was not a fearful or polite person by nature. For him to keep up his end of the mutual secrecy and pretense pact, the taboo against demanding the truth must have been potent.

The code of silence demands a lot of trust. To ask no questions about your own health, you have to trust that other people know better and mean well, whether those other people are your family or your doctor. This is something I am simply unable to do, and yet most of my relatives seem to find it easy, even natural.

During the week I spent at Akiko's house after my father's death, I began to see that she, too, was ill. The third morning of my stay, I got back from my morning run and found her sitting in the kitchen in her blue flannel pajamas. Hunched over the table with her fingers around the tea cup, she looked like someone on the verge of freezing to death.

"I don't feel very well this morning," she told me, shivering. "I'm going to lie down for a while." She unscrewed a medicine bottle, took out a couple of pills, and swallowed them with her tea.

Before I left for my run, she had been dressed in her sweater and slacks, busily dusting the bookshelves in the living room. Because she had said nothing about her own health, I assumed that while my father had not recovered from his illness, my aunt had. The first two days of my visit, my aunt had gone out with us to restaurants and coffee shops, showing no sign of being ill. But as I watched her taking her medicine that morning, I wondered if she, too, might have cancer or something equally serious.

"Are you all right?" I asked. "What's the medicine for?"

"My liver," she replied, capping the bottle and putting it back on the table.

"You still have problems with your liver?"

She nodded.

"Do you know what's wrong?" I asked.

"Oh, nothing much," she replied, smiling weakly.

"But you said you didn't feel well."

She sighed. "I don't feel that bad, but my doctor doesn't want me to get too run down. 'Anytime you feel tired,' he told me, 'go lie down for a few hours at least.' He says I can't expect to be the same as before."

What she said sounded vague, the way old people talk about their health. Akiko was only sixty-three. "How do you mean?" I pressed. "You can't be the same as before what?"

"That surgery really took a lot out of me," she said.

"But the surgery was three years ago."

Akiko poured herself another cup of tea. "At my age and with my problems," she continued after a while, "I'm lucky if I can be up and active for a couple of days and then lie down and rest the next day. My doctor tells me to be careful. 'Either you learn to take it easy at home,' he threatens me, 'or I'll make you check in and rest at the hospital.' "

Akiko went to her room, closed the door, and slept for the rest of the day—but then she got up and went to dinner with Kazumi and me. We stayed up late talking. The next day, Akiko was up before Kazumi or me; she was sweeping the hallway with her broom when I got up. She appeared perfectly healthy again.

For the rest of the visit I felt confused—I couldn't tell if she was actually ill or just run down and tired. Every Saturday she went to the hospital for tests. I asked her what the tests were for. "Nothing serious," she said, her favorite phrase in discussing her health. I had no idea what she meant. She could have been saying that she wasn't seriously ill, or that the care she was receiving was routine and acceptable, or something entirely different.

One detail my aunt repeated was that she would have to be hospitalized if the doctor didn't like the results of her weekly tests, but I didn't know what that meant, either. It isn't unusual for Japanese doctors to recommend hospital stays for patients "to rest and take it easy" whether or not they are seriously ill. After a few weeks of bed rest and additional tests, most patients are sent home without a clear explanation of what was wrong in the first place. No one complains—all assume that their condition must have improved after being under the doctor's care.

I was alarmed by Akiko's unconditional trust in her doctor. Rather than trying to understand the tests so that she, too, could consider her options, she was prepared to follow the doctor's orders—whether for surgery, hospital stay, or simply lying down in her own room, in her own house. In many small ways, I was sure, she was choosing not to know more. She used vague phrases and platitudes to cloud her own thinking. She never asked the doctor to explain the results of her tests or the reason for prescribing so many pills. I couldn't understand how she could avoid asking these questions. I would never allow anyone to take my blood without telling me what the test was for and promising to go over the results with me. I could not imagine handing over my health to someone else. Watching my aunt, I was afraid that she was giving up on herself. I would have been less puzzled if she had seemed fearful—afraid to find out the truth—but when we talked about her health, her tone was always vague but peaceful. That was what scared me the most: how calm she seemed, almost indifferent.

I saw Akiko a few times after that visit, and each time she appeared the same—cheerful and active one day, tired and pale the next. I stopped asking her or Kazumi any questions. Either they didn't know what was going on or they didn't want to tell. Only after Akiko's death—in May 1996—did I ask Kazumi, when the two of us were having dinner at a Chinese restaurant we used to go to with Akiko.

"My mother had cancer," Kazumi said, "but that wasn't what she died of. She had a swelling in her veins, which caused a lot of hemorrhaging. She got very weak. I'm sure she sensed that she wasn't going to be around very long. Since March, she kept having to go in and out of the hospital because of the hemorrhage, but the end was sudden. She didn't suffer much."

Just as Kazumi finished talking, the waitress appeared with our first course, a cream soup that was Akiko's favorite. I didn't really understand what Kazumi said. With all the details she gave me, her explanation was still oddly vague. I wasn't sure why she felt the need to say that it was not the cancer that had killed her mother. Still, I knew that Kazumi had said all she wanted to say. The most important thing she said was the last thing, "She didn't suffer much." I waited until the waitress was gone, then nodded and smiled. After a brief silence, I said it was good that Kazumi had been there to take care of her mother.

"It seems like a long time since her first surgery, though," Kazumi said, as she reached out to pour the soup from the big tureen the waitress had brought. "That was six years ago. I thought she was going to die then."

"She recovered very well after that, right?"

"Yes," Kazumi said.

After hesitating a little, I asked, "How did you know she had cancer?"

In silence, Kazumi poured the soup into my bowl. She handed me the bowl before replying, "After the surgery, the doctor said to me, 'Well, it might have been cancer, but whatever it was, it's all gone.' "

"Might have been?"

"That's how he put it, anyway." Kazumi shrugged. "I told my mother what he said, and she didn't say much about it."

I looked down at my soup—thick, yellow liquid in a white bowl—and said no more. Our spoons dipping into the bowls and scraping faintly against the sides, we ate without speaking for a few minutes before going on to other topics— my trip, the flower arrangement classes Kazumi teaches, my brother. We were two polite girls raised in Ashiya; we didn't dwell on death or illness at dinner. We had been taught to avoid saying bad-luck words like *death, sickness,* or *grief* in any conversation.

But I was upset and angry that a Japanese doctor would tell his patients that they "might have had" cancer. The polite ambiguity sickened me. I remembered hearing that in Japan, where even doctors exaggerate the hereditary nature of illnesses, people are ashamed of having cancer in the family. Maybe that's why Kazumi insisted that Akiko did not die from cancer—she was trying to protect me from worry or shame. Politeness was always a barrier in our family. My cousin and I could never be completely honest with each other no matter how close we were. Kazumi hadn't called me when Akiko was dying because she didn't want to worry me, but I wished she had chosen otherwise. If she had told me, I would have flown back to visit one last time.

Being thoroughly Japanese, Kazumi thought of pain as something to be avoided, something to protect people from as much as possible. Being only partially Japanese in my thinking, I accept facing pain as a duty I must perform to remain honest, a test of my courage or integrity. But I also understand what Kazumi was trying to say when she repeated, several times that night, "I'm so glad you were able to see my mother last year when we all had dinner in Kobe. She was still very healthy then. You were able to see her then."

One of the hardest things about living between two cultures is trying to decide what I can accept as different but well intentioned and what I cannot tolerate regardless of cultural differences. I accept my relatives' and friends' attempts to spare me a painful truth or an uncomfortable situation, even if their choice would not be mine. I can never feel the same tolerance toward institutions or society in general. Institutions that influence our health or financial well-being—and people who work for them—have an obligation to tell the truth.

In Japan after my father's death, I realized that financial information was as difficult to obtain as medical. Because my paternal grandfather, Tatsuo, had died two months before my father, my family had both estates to divide among five people: my stepmother, Akiko, Kazumi, my brother, and me. I was prepared to say that I wanted nothing if Akiko and Kazumi could have all my grandfather's money and the house in which the three of them had lived. Michiko and my brother could split my father's estate in any way. I wasn't being altruistic. I was being Japanese. Like everyone else in the family, I wanted a smooth solution without any embarrassing bickering. Even though I was sure that everyone had similar ideas about the division, I knew how hard it would be to proceed, since none of us—according to the Japanese code of politeness—could talk directly about money, a rude and crass topic to bring up among family or friends.

The one thing I counted on was that at least the banks and insurance companies would be very businesslike and efficient. I couldn't have been more wrong.

On my second day in Japan, Jumpei came over to Akiko's house to invite Akiko and me to Michiko's house. He said that Michiko wanted us to pay respects to my father's spirit at the altar and have tea with her afterward. Akiko, Jumpei, and I walked over to Michiko's. After we burned incense at the altar, Michiko asked us to sit down at the kitchen table and served us tea and melons. A few minutes later, she abruptly left the table, went to her room, and came back with some papers in her hand.

"I need your signature," she said, placing the papers on the table in front of me. She began to clear the table, plates and cups clattering in her hands.

The one-paragraph document was printed on the letter-head of a local bank. At the bottom of the page, there were three lines with my stepmother's, my brother's, and my name printed below. The lines above Michiko's and Jumpei's names already had their signatures and official seals; the last line was blank, waiting for my signature.

The paragraph, written in the very formal Japanese used only for official documents, was difficult to read. After going over it a few times in silence, I understood the gist of it:

"We, the undersigned, are the sole immediate family members of Hiroshi Mori. The balance remaining in his account, we understand, will be dispersed to only one of us, whom we choose to be our representative. If we come to any dispute later about how this money is to be divided among 'us, we will not hold the bank legally responsible."

The paragraph did not specify my father's account number or the remaining balance. There was no mention about which one of us we would choose as our "representative." With the signed letter, any of us—but only one of us—could withdraw the entire balance left in his account.

Michiko had finished clearing away the dishes and sat back down across the table from me. She was wearing jeans and a white T-shirt with a teddy bear printed on the front. I wondered if she didn't understand how ridiculous she looked or if she had dressed this way to pretend that we were having a casual family visit. She leaned forward and started off with a false, light laugh. "Stupid paper work," she said, waving her hand. "The bank won't give me any cash until the account's changed over into my name. Isn't that ridiculous? While your father was alive, I was the one who went to the bank to make deposits and withdrawals. They knew who I was and never gave me trouble. But now that he is gone, they froze the account. They won't let me withdraw any money until you've signed this statement. I can't even go to the store to buy groceries until I get more money."

I did not understand exactly how important the document was. By signing it, was I giving up my rights to a small amount of money in one of the many accounts my father had, or was all his money in this account? Would I have to sign a similar statement about everything he ever owned? What did he own anyway? I could not ask these questions without being rude and embarrassing Akiko and Jumpei.

"As soon as I get some cash," Michiko continued, "I'd like to pay for your plane fare."

"You don't have to," I said. "I came because I wanted to, not because I thought you would give me money."

I glanced over at Akiko, who was sitting next to Michiko, and at Jumpei, who was next to me. Neither of them said anything. Their faces had almost no expression at all. I read over the document again, thinking that maybe I had overlooked something. It wasn't any clearer. The document seemed bizarre. True, I was prepared to sign anything, especially if it meant making things easier for Akiko, Kazumi, and Jumpei. But how could I sign away my rights to an unspecified amount of money? Had I been naive to think that at least a bank, a place of business, would be forthright and frank? The document was as secretive and vague as everything else in Japan. It was as though even the bank thought it was rude to mention specific sums of money.

Michiko kept smiling, showing her big yellow teeth. "I'm so angry at the people at the bank," she said. "They shouldn't trouble us with paperwork at a time like this. They called only a day after your father passed away and wanted me to pick up the papers. I was so mad I couldn't go. Your poor brother had to go for me."

Looking at his signature, I suddenly understood why my brother had wanted me to come to Japan. He didn't care about seeing me. He needed me there for Michiko: he wanted my signature so that the woman he called mother could withdraw and spend our father's money. I glanced sideways at him. He didn't seem embarrassed or pained. I wanted to tell him that I felt betrayed, but I knew I would never say anything.

Instead, I picked up the pen and signed all the copies. Akiko was frowning across the table, but she didn't say anything. I had to trust that if she didn't want me to sign the papers, she would say something to stop me. Her silence meant that it was all right for me to go ahead. I pushed the signed papers across the table to my stepmother and got up to leave.

Walking away from Michiko's house, I was furious. My mother, had she lived, would have inherited my father's money. I was giving up what should have been hers and letting Michiko have it. There was no way I could get information, much less help, about what my rights were. I couldn't take my stepmother to court anyway without mortifying everyone in my family. We were supposed to be a "nice" Japanese family. None of us could take our personal or family problems to strangers like lawyers, accountants, social workers, or psychologists in Japan. Even if we lived in another city, people would find out, and our whole family would be humiliated.

The need for polite secrecy was what had made me leave the country in the first place. After my mother's death, I had lived for eight years in silence and misery. Just as I couldn't seek legal help about my inheritance now, I wasn't able, back then, to tell anyone about how my father beat me, how my stepmother made me feel like I was nothing, how I worried about my safety in their house. I didn't know any social workers, school counselors, or children's rights advocates who would interfere in the private life of our family to save me. To me, my house was like a room without doors or windows. Locked inside, I couldn't call for help or even look outside to see what help was available. Walking away from my stepmother's condominium decades later, I tried to console myself: I had been lucky enough to escape that prison, all I cared about was not going back in. The money, I told myself, was nothing.

In the week I stayed at Akiko's house and for several months afterward in Green Bay, I signed numerous forms stating my intention to renounce my rights to my father's property. None of the forms gave me specific descriptions of what I was giving up. Akiko and I had several vague and polite talks from which I gathered that Michiko would sign similar papers for Akiko and Kazumi so the two of them could have my grandfather Tatsuo's property.

In Japan—as I learned from American friends who live there—individuals don't leave wills; they express their wishes in vague and polite terms, but nothing is written down. The property laws specify how the estate should be divided among the family, strictly proportioned according to their relationship to the deceased—fifty percent for the spouse, ten percent for each child, and so forth. The law is used only when families have disputes. Otherwise, all the property goes to one person chosen by family consensus—everyone else signs forms to give up his or her legal claims, as I did. Inheritance is another example of how things are done in Japan: the public law is clear and mathematical; in private practice, families reach consensus without any open discussion.

What I hated most about my dealings with Michiko was that I was forced to act as though I trusted her. To keep the family peace, I had to sign all the papers she gave me without asking any questions or demanding to know any details. The way I was forced to act was no different from the way my relatives refrain from asking their doctors about their own health: by my silence, I was consenting not to know the truth. I had volunteered to be part of a polite lie.

Months after I returned from Japan, I kept thinking about the question of trust. Every time I went to see my doctor with a sore throat or a slight fever, I wondered if I, too, might be falling into the trap of trusting too much in doctors.

Most of my American friends think that I do. My friends in the Midwest are very skeptical about what they call Western medicine. When they have sore throats or fevers, they tend to stay home and try a combination of self-cures: vitamins or herbal medicine from health food stores, old home remedies and hot compresses. They read Andrew Weil's books and follow his advice, except for giving up coffee. Scarcely able to breathe, they still insist, "I'm sure there's nothing a doctor can do for me that I can't do for myself." If their condition does not improve in a few weeks, they finally consider looking for help, but they prefer to visit herbalists and acupuncturists rather than family-practice physicians who, they think, are rich Republicans corrupted by money and competition. One of my friends has a bumper sticker that says, I USE HERBS INSTEAD.

My American friends prefer using Eastern traditions and philosophies to prevent illnesses in the first place. They think they can stay healthy by "being in the right balance" through yoga, tai chi, Zen meditation, macrobiotic diets. They talk about the importance of breathing in a certain way to open up spiritual as well as nasal pathways. Coming from Japan, where almost nobody in my family used Eastern cures (except for a very few older relatives who took Chinese herbal supplements, but always in addition to what the medical doctors prescribed, never instead of), I do have more faith in antibiotics, flu shots, and aspirin than my American friends. The sports I learned in Japan to stay healthy were "Western" sports—running, swimming, weight lifting, basketball, volleyball. None of my twelve cousins in Japan has ever practiced tai chi, yoga, or meditation. They have no idea what macrobiotic diets are; they think only poor people eat brown rice or millet. Like me, my cousins rely on prescription drugs instead of meditation or biofeedback to get rid of migraines.

In spite of our different preferences, though, my American friends and I have something in common. We all think that trust is a matter of individual choice. My friends rebel against Western medicine just as they rebel against other Western, American, or patriotic ideas they've been taught to respect: singing the national anthem and saluting the flag, going to church, working hard to get rich. My friends don't trust these ideals or practices because they have not freely chosen them. They trust yoga and Chinese herbs because, by their own choice, they have read books and attended lectures about them. Choice and knowledge are important elements in trust.

I trust my doctor for the same reasons. I go to a doctor whose office is twenty miles away because I like the way she answers my questions—she is always clear and enthusiastic. She doesn't think that, as a doctor, she has special knowledge that I won't be able to understand, or that I should just accept her advice regardless of my feelings. I trust her, in the end, because I know she will always tell me the truth.

That's how I differ from my Japanese relatives. To me, knowledge is essential to trust. The more I know, the more I can trust. The more I can trust someone, the more I want to know their opinion. My Japanese relatives believe the opposite. The less they know, the more they rely on trust. The more they trust someone, the less they need to know. They want to trust their doctors because they think they themselves know nothing and can find out nothing. In matters of health or money, they don't ask questions because to do so is rude—it indicates that they don't trust the other person. They are willing to have no control over the two things— good health and prosperity—that are considered essential to the Japanese definition of happiness and luck.

I don't understand where my relatives' initial trust comes

from. For me, trust is something that has to be earned, something that can be lost. If I find out that someone has lied to me or kept a secret to hurt me, I will never trust that person again. With any new acquaintance, there is a period of mutual waiting—we give each other the benefit of the doubt until we can decide whether to really trust each other.

There is a clear difference between trust and faith: faith is a blind leap into the unknown, while trust has to be earned or proven over time. In Japan, every personal or professional relationship seems to require faith rather than trust. You believe in your doctor because he knows things you will never understand. You don't question your family because they know what's best for you, more than you will ever know yourself. Maybe there is something liberating about being able to assume this kind of faith—maybe it would be wonderful not to have to be guarded and skeptical all the time—but it would never work for me. I simply do not have enough faith to go around.

Japanese people place more faith in one another than in any deity. Even though almost every family visits a shrine together on New Year's Day to pray for health and prosperity, most of them admit, "I don't really believe in the gods, but it certainly won't hurt to pray." They are giving the gods the benefit of the doubt, the same way I would place tentative and probational trust in someone I don't know well.

My relatives are no exception. They wish for prosperity at Shinto shrines, pray to our ancestors at the Buddhist altar, and even celebrate Christmas—making little distinction among the deities, placing probational and lukewarm trust in all of them. The only really religious people in my family were my grandmother and my Aunt Keiko, my mother's younger sister. When I saw Keiko a few years ago, she was dying of cancer and she knew it. She talked about her condition very calmly—as Akiko did, too—but her calmness seemed clear and frank rather than polite and indifferent.

"I went to see a doctor about six months ago because I had trouble eating and I was always tired," she told me as we sat in her small living room. "I thought he was going to say there was nothing wrong with me except the normal signs of aging—after all, I am almost sixty. But the doctor kept asking me to come back for more tests, and each time I saw him, he was more vague about what the tests were for. So I knew. I knew it was something very serious, anyway."

"You knew right away?" I asked.

She nodded. "Everyone knows. It's silly to pretend."

My Uncle Kenichi and his wife, Mariko, were also in the room, as well as Keiko's husband, Mr. Maeshiba. Kenichi said to me, "Your aunt is very brave."

Keiko laughed. "I don't think so. If anything, I was a coward. I was afraid not to know. I made the doctor explain exactly what was wrong with me. I told him that it was no use trying to keep a secret from me since I had already made my husband promise that he would tell me everything."

Mr. Maeshiba nodded. "Keiko and I made a promise to each other a long time ago. If she had a terminal disease and the doctor told me, I would tell her—and she would do the same for me. We wouldn't keep a secret from each other."

"The doctor told me that I had cancer and it had spread quite a lot. I made him explain the various types of surgery and medication that were available to remove or slow down the cancer. I found out that if he performed surgery—which was what he wanted to do—he would be removing a large portion of my stomach and liver. More than likely, the cancer would keep growing, so the doctor would have to remove more later. I didn't want to be slowly chopped to death like that. I said, 'No surgery,' even though the doctor was shocked by my choice. My decision had nothing to do with being brave. I couldn't stand the idea of someone cutting me up just to prolong my life by a few months.''

She shrugged and smiled, but it took all my concentration not to burst into tears in front of her. I couldn't say anything because I was afraid my voice would crack. Keiko went on to tell me that she had asked the doctor to give her as little medication as possible. ''I don't want to be tired and forgetful, the way most people get with pain pills,'' she said. ''I don't want to be all drugged up. I want to be able to think clearly till the end.'' Then she smiled again and said, ''Let's stop this depressing talk. I have said enough.''

Her husband agreed. ''Yes,'' he said to Kenichi, Mariko, and me. ''We don't want you to visit our house and feel sad.''

Mr. Maeshiba made some tea and we ate the cakes that Kenichi, Mariko, and I had brought. For the rest of the visit, we talked about my life in Wisconsin, the recent marriages or college graduations of my younger cousins, the memories we had of my grandparents' house. We were very careful not to mention illness or death—even of other people. But it was different from the sort of pretending that usually went on in front of terminally ill people. We avoided talking about Keiko's condition because we all knew. Enough had been said about it, especially by Keiko herself—it was no secret.

On the way home in the car, Kenichi said, ''I don't think I

could face my death so easily." He stared ahead into the traffic, as if dazed. "Maybe I've been too unkind about Keiko's religion. Her faith must give her courage—but she was always a courageous person anyway. It isn't just the religion."

Keiko belonged to a religious sect called hirameki-san (a holy flash of light), one of the numerous "new religion" groups whose beliefs are based loosely on Buddhism and ancestor worship. Because the sect encourages its members to donate large amounts of money and try to convert others, my relatives were leery of it. They were embarrassed that Keiko often went to public places like train stations to hand out tracts and to preach. But everyone admitted—even before her illness—that her beliefs were harmless enough. Her sect did not promote violence, nor did it convert people against their will. Keiko spent most of her time burning incense and praying for the souls of all the dead people in our family, which was not that different from what more "normal" Buddhists did—only she devoted more time to it.

Keiko's religion must have contributed to her insistence on knowing the truth. Perhaps because she thought of faith as something sacred she devoted to hirameki-san, she did not want her doctor to play a godlike part in her life—making decisions without informing her, knowing everything while she knew nothing. She wanted to have a relationship of trust—she asked the doctor to tell her the truth so she could make decisions; once he did, she was willing to trust him to respect her wishes and not put her through unwanted surgery or medication. That is different from having faith in him. He had to earn her trust by telling the truth.

Keiko died only three months after our visit. When I heard the news, I thought of one of my earliest memories of her, from the days when I used to call her "Neine," big sister. Until I was four, my family lived in a small house in Kobe with Keiko, Kenichi, and another of my mother's brothers, Shiro. Because I was born with dislocated hips and spent my first year in a cast, I did not learn to walk until I was two. When I did finally learn, my uncles began to take me on walks to strengthen my legs, and Keiko bought me red patent leather shoes. I still remember walking around our house with those shoes on—something my mother must have tolerated even though it was against convention; we lived in a Japanese house, where the rule was to take off our shoes at the door. The tatami floor squished underneath my shoes and made me laugh. I would pretend to be on an important outing, and Keiko would give me her handbag to carry from room to room. The handbag, made of red patent leather that matched my shoes, was huge. We never put anything inside it; still, we kept opening and closing the bag, pretending to admire the invisible treasures hidden in its roomy compartments.

Years later, Keiko would stand at a crowded train station, telling complete strangers about her faith, which she must have considered to be the ultimate truth. She wasn't embarrassed to be proclaiming her beliefs, to be sharing the secrets of her happiness and peace. Faith often involves this kind of disclosure—a shouting-out of private beliefs, bringing what is hidden into light. Although I do not share Keiko's particular faith, she has set an example for me as I try to navigate my way through truths, lies, and secrets. I want to find my way out of lies and confusion. If I cannot inherit her prayers or her peace, then, at least, I want to inherit her courage to speak and hear the truth.

RITUALS

❖

In the summer of 1993, while I was visiting my friend Katie in New Mexico, the two of us drove up to Chimayo to see a miracle. The sand that bubbled up from the dirt floor of a Catholic church there, it was said, had powers to heal both physical and spiritual wounds. Although we did not believe in miracles, we thought it would be a good day-trip to drive through the mountains to visit a spiritual place.

The church, located on top of a hill, was a small adobe building. Katie and I entered the sanctuary, which looked like any small Catholic church: wooden pews, an altar with statues of saints and a cross, alcoves for candles, a stone basin of holy water. A sign on the wall indicated that the sand was in the adjoining room. We ducked under a low door beam and went into what looked like a dark storage room. The only light came through a few small windows high in the mud walls. In the corner by a wooden pillar, four or five people stood looking down at the floor. Joining them, we saw a hole in the floor the size of a large mixing bowl. The sand in the hole was lighter than the adobe floor—pale gold instead of reddish brown. A sign on the wall said, NO PIC-TURES. ONLY ONE HANDFUL OF HOLY SAND PER FAMILY, PLEASE.

Katie and I looked at each other and almost laughed, though that didn't stop us from kneeling down to scoop a handful each into the two plastic bags we had brought, just as the people ahead of us were doing. I had no doubt that the sand didn't bubble up from the floor beneath me but was brought in from the desert. I didn't mind. The ritual seemed quaint and well intentioned.

Another sign pointed to the exit—a door on the other side of the room. The wall on that side, underneath the small windows, was lined with wooden shelves. As we approached, we saw that the shelves were filled with small altars dedicated to the dead, built out of scrap metal, wood, and glass. One of them was a ten-gallon aquarium lined with pebbles and planted with miniature cacti; it had a wire mesh cover, the kind you would use to cover a hamster or gerbil cage. From the wire hung numerous silver and beaded crosses, angels, saints' medals and rosaries. On one side of the aquarium, three photographs were taped to the glass. They were wallet-sized studio portraits, all of them with the same pearly aqua background. The two photographs on the bottom were of young boys, perhaps ten and eight, both very fair and blue-eyed. They were wearing matching blue suits. The third, taped above them to form a pyramid, was a portrait of a young Mexican woman in a red dress. She appeared to be about twenty. There were no inscriptions, names, or dates. The dim light from the window was shining on the cacti inside the glass, their needles translucent like the bones of a small fish.

Katie and I left the church through the small door and found ourselves back in the parking lot. We stood by her car, blinking in the bright sunshine. I kept wondering how the three people on the aquarium were related. The boys might be brothers, but what about the young woman? She could not possibly belong to the same family. All I knew for certain was that the three people were dead and that the same person mourned them. I imagined the aqua background rolled down and stretched behind each of them at a photography studio in a small town in New Mexico. There was something timeless and placeless about the color, which was so artificially bright and pretty. Its cheerfulness made me a little sad. Even now, I remember that background as the color of grief.

On the way back to Albuquerque, Katie and I passed a cemetery where one of the graves was surrounded by a white picket fence. Inside the fence, two Harley-Davidsons, their engines removed, were chained to a rock. Colored lights and plastic roses festooned the fence and the chains. The grave looked as festive and childlike as a park or a petting zoo; the grounded motorcycles seemed so harmless, like large, dumb animals grazing in the grass.

Everything we saw that day was silly—gaudy and overdone. But sentiment isn't always tasteful. Against our better judgment, Katie and I were moved by people's desire for a miracle and by their quirky, private expressions of grief. Inspired, we decided to enact some ending rituals of our own. The two of us had met in Green Bay because our husbands, Chuck and Dean, had grown up together; they had been best friends since third grade. By the time I visited, Katie and

Dean had been divorced for nearly a year. Shortly after moving to Albuquerque together, they split up; Katie stayed on and Dean returned to Wisconsin. Though the divorce was by mutual choice, Katie still felt angry. For myself, I was thinking that I would like to be divorced, but I didn't seem to be able to work up enough energy to start such a big change. Every time I thought about it, I felt scared and exhausted. Maybe, I thought, I should get angry—anger would make me move on. This was hard since Chuck was such a nice guy. I wanted to get divorced, not because he had wronged me, but because I didn't think we were suited to each other anymore.

On the last day of my visit, Katie and I performed our moving-on ritual. In her cupboard, we found a green ceramic cup Dean and Katie had bought in the late seventies when they were newly married. Somehow, this cup came to symbolize everything we thought was wrong with Dean and Chuck, their post-hippie laid-back attitude toward life. It was an ugly cup, designed to match those avocado kitchen walls and refrigerators that were hideous even when they were in fashion. Katie and I drove up to the mountains under the shooting stars of August. We broke the cup at a camp ground, built a fire, and she burned a birthday card she had bought for Dean and never sent. "No more ugly empty cups for us," we kept chanting. We asked the spirit of change to take the anger away from Katie and pass it on to me, to get me moving. We were laughing and crying at the same time. It was ridiculous, really, and we knew it even while we were doing it.

We each took a small shard of that empty cup. For about a year, I kept mine—a green chip the size of my fingernail—in a plastic deli container with the miraculous sand from

Chimayo. Sometimes I burned incense sticks in the sand. It was my altar to something, but I'm not sure what. The ritual didn't quite work for either of us, at least not in the way we had planned. I didn't get divorced for three more years, and when Chuck and I finally split up, it wasn't out of anger. We like to think it was an odd expression of our love or respect—we were sad and relieved. I think Katie is still a little angry at Dean, but that hasn't prevented her from being happy. She is married again and has a son. Once in a while we call each other and leave messages: "Lots of change in my life, good change," "Just checking in. I hope you're happy." I imagine us twenty years from now, calling and saying the same things. Katie is a transplant like me—a Wisconsin farm girl living in Albuquerque. She knows about changes, about living between two cultures. The ritual has not been a complete failure. We could never get rid of our past with broken cups, but we have moved on.

When I saw the altars to the dead in New Mexico, I was struck by a sense of familiarity. Usually, I feel a bit out of place in Catholic churches because the objects there—the holy water, the statues, the candles—are so different from what I grew up with in Buddhist temples and Protestant churches. Those objects remind me that I am an outsider who does not know how to bless herself with the holy water and genuflect in the aisle, or when to kneel during the service, or what prayer to recite when. The church in Chimayo was different. In that dark room with scarcely enough light to see by, the altars reminded me of the Buddhist altar at my grandparents' house.

My grandparents kept their Buddhist altar in a large room

called *butsuma*, Buddha-room. A black box the size of a dresser, the altar had several shelves and drawers. On the top shelf stood a golden statue of a bodhisattva, a merciful manifestation of the Buddha spirit. On the shelf below that, my grandparents had placed four golden plaques with names and dates of the family dead—my grandfather's parents, my grandparents' two oldest children, who had died as infants. The other shelves were for flowers, incense, candles, and the small cups and bowls in which we offered food. The drawers below the shelves contained books of sutras—written in Chinese characters I could not read—and extra candles, incense, and matches.

The Buddha-room was next to the room where my mother, brother, and I slept on our futons during our summer visits. Every morning, when my grandmother offered fresh food, tea, and flowers, I got up and helped her place the bowls and cups on the shelves and light the incense sticks. Eyes closed, we prayed to the dead, asking them to protect us and bring us luck. My grandmother referred to the dead as *hotoke-sama*, the honorable Buddha-spirit, or *go-senzo-sama*, the honorable ancestors. I understood these words to mean the same thing: the spirits of all the people who had lived and died in our family, including the four whose names were on the plaques. To me, there was no distinction between the four more recent deaths and the rest, since I hadn't known any of my ancestors as living people. Even my grandmother seemed to group them together, not mourning or calling on the recently dead more than the others.

The Buddha-room was not a holy and scary place at all. During the day, our family used the room as a study. Every morning after breakfast, my grandfather and I sat at the big desk by the window to write in our journals. For a couple of hours after that, he would try to help me with math, my weak subject. I never worried that our ancestors would be embarrassed or angered by my inability to memorize multi-plication tables. For the most part, I forgot about them except when we were performing the morning ritual of offering the food and saying our prayers. They were like very old people who sat around and said nothing all day.

I don't think I was being particularly disrespectful. We were encouraged to think of our dead ancestors as benign visitors rather than holy presences. In mid-August, the time of the shooting stars, my grandparents celebrated a weeklong festi-val called O-Bon. During O-Bon, they told me, the spirits of the dead came up from the sea to visit their families. The story confused me at first because the dead were supposed to be with us every day anyway—that's why we offered them food, tea, and flowers. But I came to imagine that our morn-ing visits with them at the altar were like my mother's weekly telephone conversations with my grandmother, while the spirits' return at O-Bon was more like my family's annual return to my grandparents' house. They were two different kinds of visits.

During O-Bon, my grandparents held special ceremonies for our ancestors, inviting the monks from the local temple to read the sutras in the Buddha-room. On the last night of the week we dressed in our summer kimonos to attend the community dance held in the village square. Most of my uncles, aunts, and cousins were at our grandparents' during the summer, so we were a big group as we walked to the square, everyone taking smaller steps than usual because of the long kimonos.

In the center of the square, two or three men sat in a tall drum tower, beating on the large festival drums. There was also a singer. We danced in a circle around the tower, shuffling a few steps forward and turning sideways with a hand gesture, clapping our hands and shouting out words that made no sense, like *ah, yoi yoi* (I think this meant "yes, good, good," but I was never sure what was good). My brother, cousins, and I didn't understand the words that the singer chanted in the traditional nasal and slurred style. This was the only time during the year when we heard Japanese dance music. We just followed our relatives and neighbors around the circle, trying to make the right gesture at the right time. Some of us would invariably turn the wrong way or clap at the wrong time, and we would all giggle. It didn't matter. The music was so loud no one heard us. Our grandmother told us that we were dancing to honor the spirits of the dead, to send them back to the world of the dead for another year in peace and happiness. We imagined our great-grandparents and our great-aunts and -uncles coming back from the dead to dance with us. The weak shadows cast by the lights in the drum tower could be the dancing dead people; they were floating above us in the dark, laughing and talking about the old times. We would never be afraid of their ghosts. They were family.

Years later, when I saw an exhibit of Hmong needlework in New York, I remembered some of my childhood feelings about the ancestors. The last room of the exhibit featured burial vests and dresses, all of them hand-embroidered. The stitches were smaller than grains of sand and arranged to form complicated patterns of triangles and circles. A note under one of the glass cases explained that the patterns were particular to each clan. The Hmong trusted that when they arrived in the land of the dead their ancestors would recognize them by the clan stitches on their vests and dresses.

This belief reminded me of what my brother, cousins, and I had thought of the ancestors. They were people we had never known in life but they seemed utterly familiar. Just like our living aunts and uncles, our dead ancestors would recognize the minute details of our clothing, the shapes of our noses or eyebrows, or a particular way we smiled. "I know you," they would say. "You have our family's thin lips and big ears; that's our family crest on your kimono." Living or dead, family was the same.

The Buddhist rituals about death gave me a vague sense of comfort as a child, when I didn't know the dead. They made me feel that I was part of a big family whose members watched over one another forever. I wish I had been able to hold on to that feeling of comfort, but these days, the same rituals seem out of place when I try to mourn or at least think of the dead I know.

The morning Akiko and I went to Michiko's house to pay respects to my father's spirit, we both wore dark clothing, as was customary. She chose a navy blue suit; I wore a black sweater and dark purple pants. While my brother and Michiko waited in the kitchen, I followed Akiko down the narrow hallway that led to Michiko's bedroom.

The tatami floor was bare, with the futons folded and put away in the closet. The room didn't have much in it except for the altar against the wall by the window—a set of shelves partially covered with white cloth, taking up the entire wall. On the top shelf was a plain pine box, no larger than a shoe box, which held my father's ashes. On the other shelves, there were several incense burners, all of them sending white columns of smoke upward, a brass bell, paper lanterns, a tray of food. Incense filled my nose and mouth as I stood before the altar, staring at the tray. The doll-sized dishes and cups contained rice, pickled ginger, scrambled eggs, boiled vegetables and herbs, tea—the kinds of food I used to help my grandmother prepare for our ancestors honored at her altar. There was something wrong about seeing the dishes next to my father's ashes, as though my father, in his death, had been reduced to a good-natured make-believe spirit for whom we could leave make-believe food in toy cups.

My father did not belong in the benign white cloud of ancestral spirits I used to imagine. My relationship with him was the exact opposite of my relationship with my ancestors. After my mother's death and his remarriage, till I left home, I saw my father a few times every week, even though it was only at meals during which no one talked; some nights, we passed each other in silence in the hallway. The only time my father ever talked to me was when he scolded me and beat me. My father and I lived in the same house, ate the same food, and still we never got to know or love each other. I knew more about my ancestors than I knew about him: all through my childhood, I had heard stories about my great-grandfather—what happened when he was bitten by a poisonous snake, what a kind landlord he was. I was used to seeing pictures of my mother's two older sisters, who had died before my mother was born, and recognizing that one of them, the one photographed in a beret, looked like me. We had the same round eyes; like me, she half-frowned and half-smiled as she faced the camera. I knew nothing about my father as a child or an adult except that he was a person who drove my mother to suicide. He couldn't possibly turn into a spirit, good-natured, familiar, and yet far away.

I sat down in front of the altar, my shoulder almost touching my aunt's. She reached out and rang the brass bell to greet his spirit, just as my grandmother used to do to call our ancestors' attention to our visit. Akiko closed her eyes and bowed her head, her hands held together, palm to palm. I followed her example and closed my eyes, but no prayer came to my mind.

Are you really dead? I wanted to ask. *This can't be you.* Next to me, Akiko began to sniffle. I imagined my stepmother preparing little cups of food daily and putting them up on the shelf, as though my father's spirit were an absurd pet bird. When I thought of that, he seemed almost pitiful. Taking a deep breath, I opened my eyes and turned sideways. Akiko was pressing a white handkerchief to her eyes. Only a few years before, she had told me that my father was a strange person, that she felt scarcely related to him. I wasn't sure why she was crying. Did she pity my father now that he was dead, or was she crying because he was, after all, her brother? And what about me? Should I pity him now that he was gone? Should I tell myself that he was my father? My throat felt suddenly tight, but I didn't want to cry. My tears could only be false. Turning away from my aunt, I looked up at the wall.

Above the altar, my stepmother had hung my father's portrait. It was from ten, fifteen years before his death. His hair was still black, his face much fuller than I remembered from my visit four years ago. In the picture, he was squinting a little into the sun and smiling.

You never smiled like that at me, I thought. All I ever got from him on my last visit was a dry false laugh, a quick jerk of his head as he greeted me *hello, good-bye, see you later*—never *it's good to see you, I missed you, I've been thinking about you lately.*

My aunt was getting up. I stood up, too, and we walked back to the kitchen without speaking.

After we left Michiko's house, Jumpei, Akiko, and I went to a Buddhist temple in Osaka to visit our family grave, where my mother was memorialized. It was April, about a month past the twenty-fourth anniversary of her death. The three of us took a cab to the temple district and got off in front of a nearby flower shop.

The inside of the shop was dark. A short man in his thirties, in jeans and a white shirt, stepped out of the back room to wait on us.

"We need flowers for *hotoke-sama,*" Akiko told him, choosing my grandmother's word for the family dead: the honorable Buddha spirit. It was odd to hear this word applied to my mother. To me, *hotoke-sama* always meant a group of people I didn't know, not a single, specific person whom I still mourned. I would never be able to think of my mother as a generic and benign presence, though that was perhaps the whole point of describing her as *hotoke-sama.* My aunt had said this word to the flower shop clerk—a total stranger—as a polite and discreet way of referring to the dead without using her name and getting too personal or emotional in public. She was too polite to be anything but businesslike with a stranger.

It's impossible to think about the dead we knew without getting personal and emotional, no matter what words we use. I stood behind my aunt as the man showed us the buckets along the wall and told us that we could choose any flower we wanted. There were twenty, thirty buckets; the water inside looked dark, a heady tea of cut stems and leaves. Breathing in the scent, I felt light-headed and sad.

"We want something with pretty colors," my aunt said, pointing to the bucket of red roses. "Give me a few of those roses to begin with."

"Are you sure?" the man asked, his head tilted to one side in a gesture of doubt. "You said this was for *hotoke-sama*." It is customary to use pale, dark, or subdued colors for altar flowers—nothing too bright or cheerful.

"Oh, it's been a long time," Akiko said vaguely. "Not a recent death."

"It's for someone who loved pretty flowers," I added, stepping toward the row of buckets to join my aunt. My brother stayed behind near the door.

The man peered in my direction, shrugged, and took a stubby pencil from behind his ear. Pulling a pad of paper from his apron pocket, he waited for me to choose another flower. *The flowers are for my mother,* I wanted to say but couldn't. *I loved her.* Instead, I pointed to the bucket of pink sweet peas whose ruffled petals reminded me of the balcony at our house a long time ago—my mother had built trellises for the sweet peas to climb; hers had bloomed all summer long.

I am not sure if the rituals of mourning—building and praying at an altar, visiting the grave and offering flowers—are meant to help us express or mask our grief. Expressing something involves making it clearer, both to ourselves and to others. When a mourner in New Mexico builds an altar out of an aquarium, carefully hanging the beaded crosses, silver angels, and saints' medals from the wire cover, placing the photographs of the dead against the glass and taping them, does his grief become clearer? Whoever drove those Harley-Davidsons to a friend's grave—did they feel a sharper sense of sorrow while they took the engines apart and removed them, chained the bikes to the rock, or did the action somehow buffer them from sorrow? Can what begins as an expression of sorrow become a ritual of comfort?

When my grandmother referred to her parents-in-law and her children as *hotoke-sama*, she wasn't trying to hide her grief in front of a stranger, as Akiko was in the flower shop. To her, these people—whom she had loved once—had really joined a cloud of ancestral spirits and were no longer to be mourned individually with unresolved sorrow. Maybe after years of offering them food from her kitchen, she had transformed her grief into something milder, even comforting—a part of her daily life.

All altars—Japanese or New Mexican—do the same thing. They reduce the largeness of death into something easy to contain and tend to: small cups of food, an aquarium of crosses and medals, motorcycles that go nowhere. The altars and the graves help us parcel out the eternity of death into small daily rituals. Both in Japan and in New Mexico, the altars have doll-like or miniature features; the graves are surrounded by a picket fence or divided into concrete family plots. Mourning is a way of placing boundaries on our grief, creating a miniature replica of sorrow that we can manage.

Growing up in Japan among Japanese Buddhists, I had no idea that traditional Zen Buddhists believe in reincarnation and challenge each other with koans whose only message is "There is no easy answer. Toughen up and look into the indescribable void and work toward enlightenment, even though you can only fail." Until I met American friends who practiced Zen and read Alan Watts, I thought that all Buddhism was about honoring the ancestral spirits. Hearing the word *hotoke-sama* as a child, I never thought of its possible original Zen meaning: that at our death, we become one with the universal Buddha spirit manifested in all things. The adults who taught me the word didn't have that Zen meaning in mind. Our *hotoke-sama* ancestors watched over us and worried about our health, jobs, grades, and other particulars of our daily lives: my cousins and I were encouraged to place our grade reports (if they were good) on the altar for our ancestors to look at and be proud of. In traditional Zen teaching, even people who are alive—much less those who are dead—are supposed to transcend petty pride about their achievements.

Faith—whether Zen or Catholic—revolves around what can never be explained or made familiar. We can no more define or explain the sound of one hand clapping, our face before we were born, or why we must kill the Buddha if we encounter him on our way than we can truly understand the mysteries of the Trinity, the Immaculate Conception, or the Resurrection. Faith in its pure form demands that we leap into these unknown truths or mysteries—but this is precisely what we don't want to do when we are faced with the death of someone we love. We choose ritual over faith. We would rather string beaded crosses inside an aquarium or worship at a doll-house altar and believe that we are doing something for the dead than admit the truth—that there is nothing we can do for them, no explanations about where they have gone, whether they even exist anymore. In our grief, we cannot leap into the unknown or accept inexpressible truths. Even if our rituals seem false, clichéd, or in bad taste, they are the polite lies we need. The real miracle may be in the way ritual can turn our polite lies into truth.

In my twenties and early thirties, I had nothing but contempt for vague statements and platitudes. To say "Life goes on" instead of scrutinizing your own particular pain, I thought, was to be a coward. I didn't want to say or hear consolations like "Everyone suffers some tragedy in life" because I believed that a lame statement like that made personal suffering seem generic and trivial.

In the last ten years, as, one by one, my friends began to lose their grandparents or even their parents, I came to feel differently. Almost no one my age has any grandparents left. Now, I realize the value of platitudes. Just as we need the familiar and comforting ritual of offering food to the dead or watching cacti grow inside our aquarium-altar, we sometimes need platitudes to console each other.

Truth isn't always the best thing. Often, it is too blunt, harsh, or out of place. Several years ago, Chuck and I attended the Lutheran funeral of his maternal grandmother. Because she had many children, grandchildren, and great-grandchildren, the church was packed. The minister began his sermon in a way that we thought was promising—by talking about Hannah's life, her Norwegian family, her involvement with the Lutheran community in Green Bay, her children. "Hannah was known," he said, "for her Norwegian sense of humor." Chuck and I turned to each other and nodded, appreciating the personal touch.

But before we knew what was going on, the sermon began to take a peculiar turn. After telling one of the jokes Hannah used to tell, the minister abruptly declared, "Of course, our very faith is a joke to those who don't believe. For them, believing in God is something to laugh at." He went on about how only the saved—by which he meant Lutherans or at least Christians—could enter heaven because Jesus had gone to prepare their mansion for them. He said that Hannah was lucky to have been one of the faithful. Her family had nothing to worry about; her soul was safe with God.

In the car driving to the cemetery, Chuck said, "I should write a will. I want to be prepared. What if I died and my parents had a funeral like that? I would be so embarrassed."

"You wouldn't be," I tried to joke. "You'd be dead."

"I'm serious," he insisted. "I don't want my friends to come to my funeral and be told that they're all going to hell because they're not Lutherans."

"You're right," I agreed. "That minister should have been more sensitive. He should have expected that we wouldn't all be Lutherans. Hannah had so many children and grandchildren. He should have realized that we don't all share the same faith." I promised Chuck that I would make sure that his parents didn't have a funeral like that for him. I would hold a party in his honor and we would play his favorite music, drink beer, and tell jokes. We wouldn't even say that he "passed away," a euphemism he particularly disliked.

Hannah's funeral made me realize that I don't always want people to tell me what they consider to be the truth. Instead of telling us that only Lutherans were going to heaven, I wanted the minister to tell a polite lie: we were all going to see Hannah again in heaven regardless of our religion, so none of us should feel bad. I understood why Chuck wants his friends to have a beer party when he dies. In a typical Midwestern polite way, his friends would avoid any mention of painful truths and only tell jokes. They would comfort one another with vague and all-inclusive platitudes. No one would feel offended, hurt, or excluded regardless of religious belief.

Many times since then, I have cringed to hear harsh "truths" proclaimed without consideration. Only a few months ago, at a funeral in a small town in northern Wisconsin, a priest told the three surviving children of the deceased man, "Your mother passed away in March. It's been two months and now your father has followed. He died of a broken heart. He wanted to join your mother rather than be with you. So now, there is no family home for the three of you to come back to." Sitting in the back pew, I was appalled. The children, my friends, were only in their thirties and early forties. All of them were crying. They shouldn't have to hear that their father died of a broken heart because he would rather be dead than enjoy his old age visiting them.

"So the three of you have no home," the priest repeated before declaring that the only home they had left now was the church. "You will never be with your parents, and your childhood home is gone, but when you come to church and receive the holy communion, you will be with God in the only home you now have," he concluded.

I was angry as I left the church. The priest had no right to say the hurtful things he said, even if he had believed them to be the only and absolute truth. I wished that the sermon had offered something positive and all-inclusive. "Your parents might be gone," the priest could have said, "but their love will be with you always. You will find a home with each other and with friends who love you." Maybe statements like these are predictable and clichéd, but I wouldn't have minded hearing them.

In the face of great sorrow, I would rather hear a cliché or a platitude that may be a polite lie. When we say that someone "had a good life and didn't suffer much" or "had no regrets," it may or may not be true. But I prefer these polite lies to harsh truths—that someone's father must have died of sorrow or that someone's mother suffered terribly in the last two months of her illness. Platitudes are just like rituals. I would rather burn incense or offer food at an ugly altar than dwell on what might be the truth: the dead are beyond my ability to console them. In the same way, I would rather say and hear mild words of comfort rather than hurtful truths.

Maybe it isn't even a matter of truth versus lies. The platitudes and polite lies we say are not true in the sense of accurate, factual statements, but they make an appeal to a larger truth—the truth of our good will. We want to believe that our friends will get over their grief, that the person we loved had a good life and didn't suffer, that we will all find our homes again. Sometimes, that is precisely what does happen in the end—what we said as a platitude does become the truth. People do get over their sorrow. Just as we are comforted by the rituals of altars and offerings, we do find hope in the familiar words of solace our friends offer us.

After leaving the church where my friends' father's funeral was held, I walked across the lawn to the fellowship hall to attend the reception dinner. It was a typical Midwestern potluck of sliced ham, cheese, kaiser rolls, pickle relish, cole slaw, potato salad, Jell-O salad. Almost the whole town was gathered there, drinking coffee and eating. Old men and women went up to the surviving children to fill their coffee cups and urged them to take another brownie or lemon square. Food, I realized, was their way of saying what they couldn't, in words. They offered food and they listened.

One of the three children, Jeanne, was talking to a small group of people about her father's recent visit.

"I bought a condo last year," she said. "It's the first house I've ever owned, so my parents were very excited about it. My father was an electrician. When he came to visit me after Christmas, he rewired my condo—put in some fancy dimmer switches and things like that. Now, every time I go home and turn on the lights, I'll think of him."

I pictured her coming back from the TV station where she works, opening the door, and touching the light switch. The room would immediately fill up with light, and she would smile to remember her father putting in the new switches, hanging ceiling lights exactly where she wanted them, putting in extra outlets so she could listen to the stereo and turn on the fan at the same time. The priest was completely wrong. Jeanne has a home where she can sit in the bright light and think of her father's love.

Driving home in the dark from the funeral, I thought about my visit to my mother's grave with Akiko and Jumpei. All through that visit, I had wanted to say so much and yet was unable to. After we left the flower shop, the three of us walked in silence to the cemetery, only a few blocks away. The flowers had been arranged into two large bouquets, wrapped in newspaper. My brother carried one of the bouquets; I carried the other. Akiko walked empty-handed, her head bent a little. Although she had called my mother's spirit hotoke-sama in the flower shop, I knew that my mother would never seem like a benign and distant spirit to Akiko—no more than to me. We could never truly accept or make peace with Takako's death. I wished that there was something I could say to Akiko so she would know that I, too, was sad and would always be sad. As I glanced sideways at my brother carrying the bouquet, I wanted to tell him that my mother had loved him—just as surely as we were carrying our identical bouquets now, we were both her children. I listened to our footsteps hitting the pavement and regretted that no words would come to me. In the end, there was no way of saying what I wanted to say to them. All I could do was to walk on, carrying the flowers Akiko and I had chosen. We had named the flowers because we could not name our feelings.

A Woman's Place

❋

The spring I bought my first car I stopped at a Dairy Queen on my way home from work every afternoon. I wasn't particularly hungry for ice cream. I just liked to sit in my car in the parking lot, an ice cream cone in my hand, and watch the procession of other cars heading home. My car was like a metal-and-glass tent pitched around me. I loved being alone, claiming a little territory out in the middle of the empty parking lot. I couldn't believe that I had done without a car for so long, until I was twenty-seven.

I have a different car now, but I still feel the same way. My second car is a two-door sports car: no back seats, scarcely any trunk space. And yet when I travel, with my touring bicycle and mountain bike on the roof rack, my belongings crammed into the passenger's seat and the almost nonexistent trunk, I can hardly claim to be traveling light. My friend Don teases me about having more junk in my little car than he does in the station wagon in which he drives his three small children. "Your car is quite a habitat." he says. He is right. It's a movable home.

I never felt the same attachment to my house. A few years after I bought my first car, Chuck and I bought a house in the neighborhood we both liked. All the lots in our block had large yards with tall maples and cedars. Because no one put up fences, the connected yards made the neighborhood look like a big park. The house was just right for us: old and quaint, but in good shape so we would not have to do much work. Built in the 1920s, it was a white, two-bedroom Cape Cod—the kind of house real-estate agents describe as "a nice starter home."

As soon as I heard that phrase, I began to feel uneasy about buying the house. "A starter home" meant that we were starting something there before moving on to something else. That something was a "family," or a traditional version of it. Buyers of "a starter home" are assumed to be young couples without children. They "start" a family and, in five or six years when they have too many children to fit comfortably into a two-bedroom house, move on to a bigger place. The expression makes people sound like sourdough bread. The house is a kit or a package for multiplying dinner rolls.

Chuck and I didn't want to "start" a family. We didn't plan to have children. We were annoyed by the common assumption that now that we were buying a house, we would soon "settle down" and "raise a family." There were other expectations, too. After we bought the house, Chuck's

84

P
O
L
I
T
E

L
I
E
S

family and old friends, most of whom lived in town, began to ask us questions like, "What color is your living room?" "How will you do your bathroom?" "Are you going to change the wallpaper?" We didn't know that a living room could be identified by one single color. We ignored the questions and did what we wanted—which was to say, as little "decorating" as possible.

We were responsible homeowners. We promptly shoveled the sidewalk and driveway in the winter, cut the lawn and planted flowers and vegetables in the summer, raked leaves in the fall and put them on the curb. Chuck painted the outside of the house every three or four years and took off or put up the storm windows at the right times. But the inside of our house never had the grown-up look of other people's houses.

When we got married, we didn't have furniture because we were still in school. By the time we bought the house, we had been together for five years and we both had full-time jobs; we still slept on the mattress and box spring I had earned in graduate school by typing another student's paper. When we were finally forced to buy a new mattress two years later, because the broken springs of the old one began to stick out and stab us in our sleep, we got a futon from a local co-op and put it on top of the old box spring so we would not have to buy a bed frame. The futon stuck out from the box spring because it was a little bigger, but we didn't care: nobody saw our bed except us and the cat. The rest of the house wasn't any better. None of our dinner plates or chairs matched. We had thrown out the dining room table to make space. Chuck played his electric guitar and I used my spinning wheel in the empty room under the chandelier we always meant to replace with a ceiling fan.

For years, I didn't mind the makeshift look of our home. It began to bother me only around the time my father died, in 1993. The night I heard the news, after calling my brother and agreeing to travel to Japan, I went into our living room to sit down and relax. But as I looked around I didn't feel relaxed. The room made me think that my whole life was a mess.

Our living room was full of mismatched furniture: an ash and cherry coffee table and entertainment center made by Chuck's friend Dean, various chairs inherited from other friends or bought at garage sales. One chair had a plush rose-colored cover, while another, right next to it, was sixties earth-tone plaid. We hadn't been completely blind to the sad state of our decor. Every time we visited other people's houses, we noticed how bad our furniture was except for the coffee table and the entertainment center. In a halfhearted way, we talked about buying some "real furniture" to go with the two good pieces and throwing out the rest, but neither of us took the initiative. Getting new furniture became one of the things we talked about but never did—like remodeling the master bedroom, putting in an extra bathroom, building a sun room, looking for a summer cottage. We kept talking about the repairs and improvements we never started; we kept inheriting chairs and lamps like bad karma. Until that night, I had been resigned to our inaction. *Home-decorating isn't important to either of us,* I used to think. But that night, the state of our living room bothered me.

"Oh, this is the graduate-student, pre-baby living room

we used to have," one of our guests had said when we had first moved in. Our living room looked the same seven years later. At least in an outward way, we had made very little progress since our mid-twenties. We were stuck in a time warp of bad decor, unable to move on.

I stood in the midst of our clutter, too anxious to sit down. Chuck was upstairs in the spare bedroom, listening to music and reading. He was leaving me alone because my father's death was a shock and I didn't know what to make of it. In times of confusion, I never want to talk—I want to be alone. Chuck was doing the right thing by giving me space, being considerate. Just for a moment, though, I wanted to run upstairs and tell him that we needed to make some changes and start living like adults—but I wasn't sure what that would mean or why I felt the need to say it. So I sat down on the couch—the only item we bought new, beige to match our cat so his hair wouldn't show even if we didn't vacuum very often. Closing my eyes, I took a deep breath and tried to prepare myself for the trip ahead—for acting like an adult in Japan even though my American home was like an overgrown dorm room.

Chuck and I couldn't decorate our house partly because we were rebelling against our parents' houses. He grew up in a small house divided into three bedrooms, a kitchen, a dining room, and a living room; each room was decorated with wallpaper, borders, painted trim, furniture and lamps that matched. After Chuck and his siblings left home, his parents converted one of the bedrooms into a den; every couple of years, his mother redecorated, changing the color scheme or the style of the rooms. She once had a dream about wallpapering the inside of the toilet—she had to cut and paste the paper just right.

Chuck got along well enough with his parents, but he didn't want to live in a house that was just like the one he had grown up in. Because his parents' house had been divided into small rooms full of furniture, he wanted ours to have a lot of "open space"—a dining room without a table, a master bedroom without a bed frame, a spare bedroom that had only a desk and a couch. He liked our rooms to look spare and open, to have an almost Eastern feeling.

While he tried to pare down our belongings and open up more space, I was working hard to clutter that space, to make it more comfortable. I had lived with my father and stepmother in a Japanese house that didn't have clear boundaries. Though my own room was Western-style with a regular door, carpeted floor, and a bed, the rest of the house had sliding fusuma doors that were kept open most of the time so that one room emptied into another. Everyone else in my family slept on futons that were put away during the day. Open doors and empty spaces reminded me of how scared and lonely I used to be: the only place where I felt safe in that old house was behind the closed door of my bedroom. So when I had my own house, I continued to mark off small territories of my own with stacks of books, plastic cartons of my spinning, weaving, and knitting supplies, piles of sweaters that didn't fit into closets. I insisted that we keep all the living-room furniture people had passed on to us. Our separate rebellions left our house looking minimalist and cluttered at the same time.

I often envied Chuck because his "baggage" about home-ownership seemed much lighter than mine. When we went to feed his mother's cats while his parents were away, he would always open the refrigerator and drink a soda or eat the candy his mother kept in glass dishes. In their living room, there was a big studio portrait of the four children, taken when Chuck was in first grade. I made fun of the portrait because everyone's ears looked too big, but I was jealous. For Chuck, his old house was still a place of free food and drinks, a place where his parents proudly displayed pictures of him. I could not imagine feeling so comfortable in my parents' house; after my mother died, no one in my family ever took a photograph of me.

In another way, too, I thought Chuck had it easy. Being a man, he rebelled only against his own past, while I was up against something bigger. In both Japan and Green Bay, a woman's place is considered to be inside her house. I resented the expectation that it was my job—not Chuck's—to "make a nice home" for us by decorating, cooking, and cleaning.

Everyone who asked Chuck and me about home decorating addressed me more than Chuck. They made eye contact with me and directed their questions to me, not him. When we were at parties and someone talked about buying furniture or a new appliance, many of the men said they left the final decisions up to their spouse. "My wife chooses and I pay," they said, laughing in a proud and manly way. In small towns in the American Midwest, household tasks are divided by gender. Women are supposed to take charge of anything decorative, aesthetic, and superficial, leaving their men to deal with the more important decisions about finances or overall structure. Many women choose their husbands' new clothes as well as the wallpaper, the furniture, the color and the style of the new appliances for their homes. But if the house needs a new roof, a new furnace, or a large structural repair, their husbands are in charge of assessing the damage, calling the right kind of repair people, and negotiating with them.

Owning a house made me more aware of these stereotypes. When Chuck and I were living in an apartment, people didn't expect us to be like other married and settled couples. They didn't ask me about furniture, so I didn't know that many people expected me to be more interested in house decoration than in writing, teaching, or running. Once I knew, I couldn't get over feeling angry and belittled. People talked as though, in all areas of life, women were more interested in surface decoration than content. When my friend Diane, a philosopher married to another philosopher, mentioned having helped her husband write his books, even some of our colleagues at the college assumed that she had proofread his manuscripts and suggested stylistic changes. They looked surprised to hear her husband say that Diane had helped him examine his basic concepts by challenging the weak links in his arguments. Talking about marriages and houses seemed to bring out everyone's sexism.

When Diane was teaching part-time at our college—where her husband teaches full-time—she ran into someone from work while she was shopping. Her arms loaded with sweaters, she was looking for a fitting room. The man smiled at her, winked, and said, "Out spending your husband's money?" She nodded curtly and kept walking—when she got to the fitting room and closed the door, she realized that she was holding back her tears.

I understood how Diane had felt. She had been too shocked by the man's comment to respond or to correct him. What distinguishes unjust discrimination from other forms of rudeness may be that we never get used to it: every time, we are shocked and appalled as if it were the first time. I had known about sexism before Chuck and I bought a house. But reading books, attending women's studies classes, or watching interviews on TV never prepared me for experiencing it myself. Every time someone asked me if I ironed Chuck's shirts, if I planned to work part-time or stay home once we had children, I wanted to cry or slam the door and walk out. I never got used to being reminded that I was "just a woman" and that a woman's place was in the house. I couldn't help seeing the house as something that was used to put a woman "in her place"—a form of punishment.

If gender discrimination were something we could get used to, I would have been well prepared long before I bought a house. In Japan, a woman's place is always in the house, which belongs to a man. The most common Japanese word for a wife is ka-nai, literally, "house inside." It is a word that a man uses to refer to his own wife, not to someone else's (the word for that is okusan, "an honorable person in the back"). In contrast, a woman refers to her husband as shu-jin, which means "master," "a person in charge."

Because these words, along with most people's first impressions of Japan, imply that men are considered far superior to women, Americans and other "foreigners" are often surprised to discover that in everyday practice men are not in charge of their homes or families. In most households, wives control the family finances and make both large and small decisions that influence every member of the family. Japanese men turn over their paychecks to their wives, who give them small monthly allowances. The wife decides which house the family will buy, what furniture or appliances they will purchase, where their children will go to school. Some wives lock their husbands out if the men return home too late after a night of drinking. A drunken husband is not fit to come into the house.

In a way, Japanese wives are more truly "in charge" than their American counterparts. No man in Japan would say, "My wife chooses the furniture and I pay," because the money belongs to the family, not to him. If a roof needs to be repaired or an addition has to be built, a Japanese woman contacts the repair people and negotiates with them herself. She doesn't expect her husband to be the spokesman for the family. A Japanese wife does not merely decorate her house and wait for her husband to make sure that it is structurally sound. Even the Japanese pictorial character for *safety* is composed of parts suggesting "a woman under a roof." It is a woman, not a man, who gives a sense of security to a house in Japan.

But when I think of the Japanese women I know—my mother, my aunt, my friends from school—I understand that being in charge is not the same thing as having power or freedom. A person can be in charge of her house and still be trapped by it. As a mainstay of the family, a Japanese woman is expected to work hard and to make many sacrifices. Everything she does is for the good of the house and her family (the word *ie* means both a house and lineage or family), not for her own pleasure.

When I stayed at my Aunt Akiko's house in 1993, I understood why I was always turning up the heat in my house in Green Bay and cluttering up the space with yarn and books. I was trying to make sure that my house didn't become a cold, comfortless place like the Japanese houses in which I had grown up. Akiko's house was one of those houses. My family lived there for a year with my grandfather when I was in kindergarten; my brother and I also stayed there for a month after our mother's death.

Coming back to this house as an adult, I couldn't get over its lack of warmth. One morning after Akiko had gone back to bed to rest, I sat in the kitchen trying to read a book. Though it was a sunny, warm April morning, the kitchen was dark and cold. Like many old Japanese houses, Akiko's house was designed to stay cool during the hot summer months; it had large windows and most of the rooms faced north or were shaded by trees and an outside wall. Maybe for the two hot months of the year, these features made the house a comfortable place, but for the other ten months, the house was dark, drafty, and cold. There was no central heating. The only heat came from small electric space heaters placed in a few of the rooms. Even with the heater on, the kitchen was freezing.

I considered going upstairs, where it would be a little warmer, but there would be no place to sit. The three upstairs rooms were the traditional tatami-floor bedrooms with scarcely any furniture. During the day, when the futons were folded up and put away, the rooms were empty. There were no chairs or couches. I couldn't sit around reading in bed in the middle of the day, as I sometimes do at my house in Green Bay when I want to spend a relaxing afternoon.

Except for the kitchen, the only room that had chairs was the formal drawing room downstairs, the coldest room in the house. The couch and the chairs there were stiff and uncomfortable. My grandfather had used the drawing room only for guests; we didn't sit there ourselves even on special holidays. I stayed in the kitchen, hunched over the book with my hands tucked inside my sleeves.

To many Japanese women who stay home all day their houses must seem oppressive—not a sanctuary from the outside world or a place of rest, but a place that drives them to hard work and sacrifice. Many upper-middle-class women, like my aunt, spend their days in cold kitchens, and yet they don't renovate their houses and put in central heating, which they can surely afford. They will not spend money on something that would benefit only themselves. Their husbands and children, who follow typical Japanese work and school schedules, are seldom home except to sleep. Having a warm house all day long is not an important concern for them, so the women choose to put up with the cold. "It's just me at home all day," they say. "It's not important." The women don't have a lot of time to sit around anyway: there is so much work to do, and they reason that working will keep them warm.

My aunt, a typical Japanese housewife, never sat down to relax for more than ten minutes unless she was ill. For her, to be in the kitchen was to be at work. She was always getting up and cleaning the sink, washing the few dishes that we had just used, or sweeping the floor once again. Even though my cousin and I wanted to help, she would not hear of it. Working alone was a habit with my aunt. She and most women her age—and many younger women, too—lived all their lives with men who never washed dishes or even boiled water for their tea. These men expected to be waited on once they were home from work. The children, too, were supposed to spend their time studying, not helping their mothers around the house. The women were left alone to do all the work, and yet what they did left no trace. They were constantly cleaning the kitchen to erase any sign of their hard work—dropped crumbs, scattered tea leaves, peeled vegetable skins.

An ideal Japanese woman effaces—rather than expresses—herself. She is valued for her ability to pretend that her hard work is nothing, that she is scarcely there. The home she creates is a pure, empty space. Its beauty is elegant but cold. My aunt's sparsely furnished kitchen didn't reflect her personality or taste. The walls were bare except for a calendar from the paint company my grandfather had owned and a small Shinto shrine that had been put up to guard his health. Even though he had been dead for a few months, he seemed more present than my aunt or my cousin. I missed the kitchens of my neighbors or in-laws in Green Bay with the potpourri, scented candles, and country-decor hearts and geese I thought I despised. I wished I hadn't made fun of the things people had put in their homes to express their taste or personality. Anything seemed preferable to the emptiness of my aunt's house.

I also missed my living room with its mismatched furniture. No matter how bad our furniture was, our house was still a home. In all the rooms, there were places to sit and relax: watch television, listen to music, talk, read. Chuck and I had put up our friends' artwork and posters of our favorite museum exhibits. The shelves were full of our books and music cassettes and CDs. Anyone who visited us would learn something about our tastes, interests, hobbies. Our house in

Green Bay didn't reflect the Japanese ideal that a woman should go through her life taking care of other people, leaving no trace of herself. Both Chuck and I were leaving plenty of marks on the space we occupied.

Sitting alone in my aunt's kitchen at night during my visit, I thought about my mother. When my family lived in that house, my mother stayed up late after the rest of us had gone to bed—my brother and me upstairs, our grandfather in the downstairs room. Even back then, my father was seldom home. He had a lover in another town, and he often went to stay with her, leaving my mother to take care of his father. Although he used his business trips as excuses, my mother knew the truth. Sitting in the same kitchen thirty years later, I wondered if she had sat up late because she was angry. Did she think about her husband and the other woman and cry? Or was she trying to relax, to enjoy her solitude in the few quiet hours she had to herself to read or work on embroidery—to do something she liked? All day, she was busy taking care of my brother and me. As soon as my grandfather came home from his paint company, there were constant demands from him: he wanted tea, clean clothes, supper, more tea. If he spilled a drop of water on the table, he did not wipe it himself but called her to clean it up. "Takako, Takako," I remember his voice, nagging and scolding.

I was sorry that she'd had no place but the dark, cold kitchen to sit in. I hoped that she had been happy to have some time to herself after everyone else went to sleep. Surely, I thought, she could not have been sad or angry every time she was alone. But it was hard to feel cheerful or hopeful in that kitchen. My cousin had left the flowers she had been arranging: flowering branches of plums mixed with some annuals, anchored by a cluster of needles at the bottom of a shallow vase. The flowers were the only decoration in the house. Kazumi bought a large bucket of mixed annuals every week, arranged them in several vases scattered around the house, and then replaced them the next week. Though they were beautiful, the flowers didn't cheer me up—I wished Kazumi would make something that would last, a painting or a quilt we could look at ten years later and say, "Remember when you did that?"

Kazumi was thirty-six, about the age my mother had been when she lived in the house. Kazumi and my mother were very much alike. Just like Kazumi, my mother had shoulder-length hair; she arranged flowers for no special occasion, resigned herself when she didn't get what she wanted, and went on smiling and taking care of other people until she couldn't bear her unhappiness. Kazumi and my mother both tried to live up to the age-old ideal of a nice Japanese woman. The friends I grew up with, I was sure, were doing the same thing—carrying on our mothers' legacy of patience and beauty and consideration. I wondered if most of them were happy or lonely or both. I imagined my friends staying up late, trying to enjoy their moments of solitude and yet feeling lonely. Sitting in front of the tower of flowers my cousin had made, I thought of all the women driven to be alone late at night, craving solitude and yet lonely for a different life; night after night, they practiced flower arrangement or embroidery—disciplines of beauty against so much sadness.

My mother had many reasons to sit alone in the kitchen feeling miserable. My parents' marriage didn't get any better after we moved out of my grandfather's house into our own apartment or even after my parents had bought a house of their own. When I was in fourth grade, my father's first lover, Okiyo-san, started calling our house late at night, looking for my father. When my mother said that he was not home, Okiyo-san told her that my father was cheating on them both with a new lover. Soon, the new lover—Michiko—found out about Okiyo-san and took to calling our house when my father wasn't with her. As my mother sat alone in her kitchen, she could not even look forward to being left in peace: one of the women would call to weep and complain about my father's unfaithfulness.

I remember the phone ringing late at night and my mother being upset afterward, but I hadn't known the exact details until after my father's death, when my Aunt Akiko told me. Until then, I had assumed that my father had had an affair only with Michiko, and that all the late-night calls had been from her.

"Oh, no," Akiko said, "Okiyo-san was his lover long before Michiko. She was the woman who lived in Mizushima."

We were sitting in a coffee shop in Osaka, near the family cemetery where we had visited my mother's grave. Watching the men and women drinking their coffee, cigarette smoke curling toward the ceiling, I remembered something I had almost forgotten.

"She lived in Mizushima?" I asked Akiko. "Is that the woman who used to send us peaches?"

Akiko nodded.

"I remember those peaches," I told Akiko. "I had no idea that they were from my father's lover."

"Your father was seeing Okiyo-san long before you two

were born," Akiko told my brother and me. "She lived in Mizushima and owned a bar your father went to when he was in town on business. That's how he met her. Pretty soon, he was telling all his friends from work to visit the bar when they were in Mizushima. 'She's a special friend of mine,' he told them, making no secret of their affair. After your mother was gone, he would have married Okiyo-san if she hadn't already been married. She had a husband, though he was seldom in town because he was a sailor. Okiyo-san wanted to divorce him and marry your father, but your father couldn't risk his reputation by marrying a divorced woman. He married Michiko even though she had only been his lover for two or three years instead of fifteen or sixteen." Akiko sighed and shook her head. "So I guess for a while before your mother's death, your father had two lovers. Your mother said that both of them called the house and got upset if he was gone—your mother was laughing and crying at the same time when she told me. 'Now I've got two women looking for him,' she said."

Okiyo-san's peaches arrived at our house every August, in a big wooden box wrapped in brown paper. My mother told my brother and me to be careful. "Make sure you wash and peel those peaches," she nagged us. "My sister Etsuko died from dysentery. The last thing she ate before she got sick was an unwashed and unpeeled peach. I don't want you kids getting sick."

I always wondered why my mother was so cautious about those peaches. No one died from dysentery anymore. My mother didn't insist on washing or peeling other fruits—she often saw my brother and me taking big bites out of unpeeled apples and pears and said nothing.

After what my aunt told me, I finally understood. To my mother, peaches were contaminated—reminders, not of her sister's death, but of her own humiliation and my father's betrayal. I wished my mother had taken the whole box of peaches and smashed them against our doorstep. She could have refused to buy or eat peaches forever and forbidden Jumpei and me to touch them. Instead, my mother carefully sliced and cored each fruit, removing the fuzzy pink skin with her paring knife. She put the wet yellow slices on a pretty plate, swallowed them with her tears.

Like most Japanese women, my mother was in charge of our house but was expected to act like a servant when there was company. From time to time, my father brought his work friends to our house after the bars closed so they could continue their drinking and talking in our living room.

As expected, my mother served the liquor and snacks and then retreated into the kitchen, letting the men talk and drink undisturbed. She reappeared only to refill their glasses and dishes, not to join in the conversations. Nobody spoke to her or asked her how she was. It must have been humiliating for her to sit in the kitchen listening to their loud laughter. Everyone knew about my father and his lover. Many of the men must have visited Okiyo-san's bar with my father and seen the two of them together. When my mother went in to refill their glasses, she was having to do exactly what her husband's lover did.

On those nights, my brother and I were already asleep. The few times my father was very drunk, he woke me up and insisted that I play the piano for the guests. I would play two, or three pieces and go back to bed—saying good night to my mother, who was alone in the kitchen preparing snacks for the guests. Though I don't remember seeing her serve the food and the drinks, I know one thing about my mother: the more cheapened she felt, the calmer and more poised she would have behaved, tilting the beer bottle and the glass at just the right angle to make a perfect crown of foam. It would never have occurred to her to drop the glass on purpose on someone's lap or to spit into my father's drink in secret.

My mother was a sweet, gentle person, her friends and family always tell me. They remember her, as I do, as a beautiful and sad woman. I loved her poise, her gracefulness. But I want to be different. I don't want grace or beauty if it means turning all my disappointments into something spare and elegant, an artful silence. I don't want to live my life in quiet dignity.

I decided to be divorced because I began to sit alone in the kitchen late at night, as sad and silent as my mother had been. Yet there was a big difference. Chuck had never caused me to be unhappy: he would never lie to me, hurt me, or belittle me. Unlike my parents, we spent a lot of time together and were happy when we were together. We talked and laughed a lot—about politics, work, religion, books, other people. I could not imagine a life in which I didn't talk to him every day.

But something was wrong. If Chuck didn't make me unhappy, then our marriage did. What each of us wanted to do with the house applied to our lives as well. Chuck wanted to pare down his life and open up more space, while I wanted clutter and comfort. Because he was from Green Bay, Chuck already had a few old friends from childhood. He hadn't made new friends at work, but he didn't mind. When he was younger, he said, he enjoyed spending time with a big group of friends, but now he appreciated being alone with me. He was ready to settle down a little more. We should move to a large house out in the country, he said—we would build a house in a big lot and never be bothered by neighbors. We would have a lot of space where we could be alone.

The idea of living in the country frightened me. I liked living in town, within a few blocks of grocery stores and coffee shops. After ten years in Green Bay, I finally had close friends from work and from the various volunteer or arts-and-crafts groups in town. For the first time in my life, I belonged to a community of like-minded people, and that was important: I had grown up feeling lonely because my Japanese friends and I had so little in common; I had spent my twenties and early thirties with friends I could not keep because people were always moving on. Now that I was finally settled into a community, moving to a house in the country with just my husband sounded like a return to loneliness. I wasn't ready for that—I would never be.

A house in the country, I was certain, would feel like a trap. No matter how nice Chuck was or what a good relationship we had, I would end up feeling as lonely and miserable as my mother had. If I had to choose between living alone but having many friends and living with a husband but having no friends, I would have to choose the first.

From time to time Chuck and I talked about our differences, but our talk always petered out, just like our plans for house renovation. We didn't have ugly fights and we didn't get angry at each other, but we could not resolve anything. Our house matched our marriage: nothing was really wrong and yet we seemed stuck in something that wasn't quite right, doomed never to move on.

No matter what we decided, one of us would have to make a sacrifice if we were to stay together. Either we lived in town and socialized more or we lived in the country and spent more time alone. I didn't want to give up anything I wanted, but when Chuck finally told me that he would be willing to make a compromise and just move to a bigger place in town, I was suddenly scared. All our lives together, we would have to remember how he had given up something for me. A future based on his sacrifice was like a bottomless pit I could fall into, never to come up. I didn't feel any better knowing that Chuck wouldn't blame me or resent me; he wasn't that kind of person. We might both be happy in a new house in town, and he would never remind me of what he had given up for me, but it would still be wrong. What was wrong with us, in the end, was not our disagreement about where to live. We could never move forward together because I was incapable of making or accepting sacrifices. If marriage meant sacrifice, mutual or one-sided, I wanted to be alone.

I went to live in a small studio I had been renting for a few years as a work space. Chuck had wanted us to have a big house in the country where I could have a quiet and comfortable writing room. As I unpacked my boxes in my studio, I felt sad that he had imagined a nice room for me in his vision of our house together, but I knew that I could never have lived in that house even if I had a private room. Because I had been using the place as a work space, the studio already had some of my things. Moving in, I had the same sense of comfort I experience when I go to a store and buy clothes that look just like the ones I already have—everything seems right, meant for me, and I can't imagine anything different.

It could be that some of us reenact the same space over and over in different apartments. My small kitchen is just like all the kitchens I have lived in since I left my parents' house—the same plates and utensils arranged in pretty much the same way. The exposed bricks and warped window frames give my studio the temporary and makeshift look of the house I had just left. My books and yarn clutter the three tiny rooms. But the big windows overlook the only truly busy street in town, with its several coffee shops and two bookstores. Living in my studio is a lot like sitting in my first car in the Diary Queen parking lot: I am alone in the midst of traffic, and somehow that gives me comfort—to be alone and yet to be part of something larger.

My studio is upstairs from a photography studio where people get their high school graduation or wedding pictures taken. Most of them arrive casually dressed, with several dresses or suits packed into their gym bags. Walking in or out of my studio, I often see these people outside—standing in front of the brick façade of the building and brushing their hair or reapplying their lipstick between shots.

Watching people trying to look their best, I am reminded of the beauty salon my mother and I used to visit when I was a child. The salon, like my studio, was a small place in an old building overlooking traffic. Its large windows had a view of a busy street lined with shops, and across that street, a train station. My mother and I went there once a month to get our hair trimmed.

Arriving at nine or ten in the morning, we walked up to the receptionist, who sat at a large metal-top desk at the entrance to the room. She would hand us pink gowns to put over our clothes before seating us in two of the chairs in front of the wall-to-wall mirror. The salon was one big room with large windows in the back. Along the opposite wall from the mirror, a few women sat in identical pink gowns under the round dryers shaped like space-age helmets. Reading magazines and sipping fruit drinks, the women looked as though they were traveling to Mars or the moon.

The hair-dressers, who were all young women dressed in white gowns, complimented me on my long hair. They fussed over my mother and told her how young she looked. She was so beautiful, they said, that a little lipstick and the simple shoulder-length haircut were enough to set off her looks. My mother and I smiled and made mildly disparaging comments about ourselves, so no one would think we were vain. I knew everyone received a compliment—being flattered was part of getting a haircut. But there was no need to be on our guard. My mother *was* beautiful. When someone praised her beauty and she denied it with a smile, I could see that the exchange gave both of them a good, friendly feeling. Sometimes the other women who were getting haircuts joined in the conversation, and all of them chatted and laughed as they talked about shopping or TV or their children.

For my mother, the beauty salon was the opposite of the kitchen. It was one of the few places where she was pampered and complimented, where she didn't have to take care of other people. Instead of being alone, she was with other women. Though she didn't know these women by name, they were regular customers at the same salon, so they didn't have to treat one another with the polite silence of strangers. Dressed in identical pink gowns, they sat together like reunited school friends or cousins, talking about nothing important but feeling cheerful and friendly.

My mother was happier in rooms that weren't her own. The public places that we visited together seemed more intimate and comfortable than the cold houses in which we lived. Every month she and I went shopping downtown or visited the art galleries in Kyoto to see exhibits. We stood in room after room full of paintings or bolts of fabric or dresses, admiring what we saw and talking to each other. If we got tired, we found tearooms where we could rest and drink tea or coffee in pretty cups. We felt so comfortable in these rooms—though they were public places, I felt they existed just for us. My mother showed me that it was all right to be made happy by the small, seemingly trivial things like clothes and haircuts and compliments as well as by works of art. She made me feel that the whole city was my home.

For her, a woman's place was the city itself, not her house. I know that my life can be—and already is—different from hers. Maybe someday I will have a house again and a big garden that will remind me of a park. The summer after Dean and Katie were divorced, I visited their old house and saw the roses and salvias Katie had planted. They were leafing out and blooming again in her raised beds, and they seemed like the saddest things I could see. For many summers, my lavender and delphinium, too, will keep on flowering without me. It's as if the lives we've chosen not to live had gone on without us, a small pantomime in the corner of a garden. Doing the right thing doesn't mean that we have no regrets. Still, I love the temporary home I have made in an almost public place, staking out a little private space in the midst of traffic. It's a good place to be.

CHAPTER SIX

BODIES

※

A few years ago, I got together with some friends from work to trade old clothes. Each of us brought shopping bags full of dresses, blouses, skirts, and pants that were in perfect condition but didn't fit or were no longer our style. We met at one of our houses, had a potluck lunch, and went up to the large bedroom upstairs to try on the clothes. There were six of us. We had put the garments on the bed; they made quite a pile. The first two women who found something they liked stepped into the corner, turned their backs to the rest of the room, and began to change.

I wasn't at all embarrassed to see them in their undergarments. These were women I knew pretty well; I swim at the Y and change in the locker room with women I don't even know. Modesty shouldn't be a concern among friends. The clothes I wanted to trade were the dresses and skirts from my first semester as a college professor, before I realized that no job was worth looking so unlike myself. They fit my friend Cheryl, who looked much better in them than I ever did. Another woman made fun of me in a good-natured way, saying, "I can't believe you wore these. You must have been really nervous about your job."

Because I was having a good time, I didn't notice right away that one of the women was sitting in a chair in the far corner, not trying anything on. When the rest of us asked, she claimed not to have found any clothes she liked. She wasn't rude. She politely complimented other people from time to time. But sitting stiff-backed and cross-legged, she looked uncomfortable. Her cable-knit sweater, wool skirt, and thick brown boots seemed oddly bulky. In the meantime, another woman, who was a body-builder, began prancing around, saying that she looked fat and ugly so that someone else would say, "Are you kidding? You look gorgeous." While the rest of us changed near the wall or in the corner, our backs turned to one another, the body-builder walked around nearly naked and then stood changing in the middle of the room. I found myself going as far away from her as possible to change. She made me nervous.

A week later, I had coffee with my friend Diane, who had been at the clothes exchange. I wanted to know what she thought about the odd behavior of the two women.

"Wasn't that kind of weird at Maggie's house?" I asked in a vague way because I wasn't sure if Diane had noticed the same things I had.

Diane nodded. "Yes, I felt so bad for Vivian. She didn't have to sit in the corner feeling uncomfortable like that."

"I know," I agreed. "If she was really embarrassed to change in front of us, she could have asked to use a different room. We wouldn't have been offended."

"I wish she hadn't felt so uncomfortable, though," Diane said. "We're good friends. We weren't there to judge her. Of course we all hate our bodies, but we all understand that."

Stunned by what she said, I joked that our body-builder friend probably didn't hate her body.

"I think she does, too," Diane said. "That's why she's so insecure and has to be so vain."

"Maybe you're right," I nodded.

People who are vain are often insecure, so what Diane said about the body-builder made sense, but I was taken aback by the matter-of-fact tone in which she had said, "We all hate our bodies." I thought of the six of us changing in that big bedroom. It had never occurred to me that we all felt that way. We were six women in our thirties and forties, all of us in perfect health, none of us overweight, underweight, missing any toes or fingers, or having anything out of the ordinary that might make us self-conscious. Except for the body-builder, who was very beautiful, the rest of us looked mildly attractive in an unremarkable way: people wouldn't turn their heads to stare at us out of admiration or disparagement. We had no reason to hate or love our bodies.

Diane is one of the most thoughtful people I have ever met, so it seemed odd that she would feel insecure about something that didn't bother me at all: I never thought much about my body in one way or another. I care about my health, but I don't dwell on the shapes and the sizes of various parts of my body, the way many American women seem to. My attitude toward the body is more pragmatic, I realized, because I grew up in Japan. I was spared an American upbringing that teaches women that their bodies are sexual objects about which they should feel guilty or inadequate. In Japan, the body is not the inferior part of the body-soul dichotomy. It isn't so heavily associated with sex, sin, guilt, or love. For a Japanese woman growing up in a polite upper-middle-class family, the body is desexualized. Maybe, I thought, that is something I should feel thankful about.

Even the word *body* in English sounds heavy and portentous—the broad *o*, the solid *b* and *d*. It's one of the words we think of in pairs: body and soul, black and white, heaven and hell, good and evil. Words that come in pairs usually suggest a conflict or need for choice. The commonly used Japanese word for the body, *karada*, does not have the same associations. The word has connotations of health rather than those of sin or sex. *Karada* ni *yoi* means "good for one's health"; *Karada no choshi wa yoi* means "My health has been good" even though, literally, the sentence says, "My body has a good pace." *Karada ni ki o tsukete*, people advise each other as a form of farewell: "Be careful with your body." It's a casual expression, just like "Take care of yourself." There is nothing personal or intimate—much less sexual—about these references to the body in Japanese. In English, I would not say to people who aren't close friends, "My body has been acting up," because any reference to the body seems too intimate. It is more polite to say, "I haven't been feeling very well" or "My health has been poor." In Japanese, the word *karada* simply does not have the same feeling of taboo.

Growing up in Japan, I thought of my body, my *karada*, as something practical that I had to take care of by gargling, getting enough sleep, and eating the right foods. There were plenty of things we were forbidden to talk or think about—

even a reference to how we really "felt" or what we "wanted" was usually unwelcome—but the body was not on the long list of taboo subjects. That is not to say that we acted in an uninhibited manner. My friends and I were modest. None of us wore low-cut dresses or rode on trains in halter-tops and miniskirts. Nobody wanted to. Showing off one's body seemed like a bizarre and embarrassing form of behavior, rather than a forbidden and daring adventure. For the most part, we acted as if—and believed that—our bodies scarcely existed except when something went wrong with our health so we had to think about stomachaches or sore throats or sprained ankles.

Our attitude toward sex was similar. We didn't have sex education classes, but our tenth grade biology class had a unit on reproduction. By that time, we all knew "the facts of life" through hearsay or movies or magazines. The biology lessons didn't give us any new information. The lectures were dry and abstract. There wasn't any discussion. Human sexuality seemed as unrelated to us as the genetics of different colored beans or peas we had to memorize.

My friends and I had no language to speak about sex, in or out of the biology class. Even the few articles we found in women's and young girls' magazines used English words for anything related to sex—*sex, penis, orgasm,* etc. To this day, I am not sure what the original Japanese words for these things are, if such words exist at all. The borrowed English words gave an impression that sex was something that happened only in foreign countries or on another planet. None of the articles gave practical advice or encouraged discussion. They seemed just as abstract and faraway as the biology lessons.

My American friends—especially those who grew up in

Catholic families—recall feeling confused about sex through-out their adolescence. One of them still remembers the sex education classes that were taught by priests. "I think some of those priests enjoyed talking about sex, in a sick kind of way. They went into a lot of detail," he says. "So my friends and I knew everything about sex, and everything was forbid-den. We felt scared and guilty." My experience at my Japa-nese girls' high school was the exact opposite. My friends and I knew the scientific facts about reproduction, but no-body thought or talked about how these facts applied to our own bodies and lives. Sex didn't have the allure of a forbid-den subject. It was something we were too well-bred to worry about.

This polite denial of sexuality wasn't all bad when my friends and I were teenagers. It kept us out of trouble with-out making us feel rebellious. We never considered becom-ing sexually active, not because it was a sin or an immoral and forbidden act—as many of my American friends were taught—but because the consequences could only inconve-nience and embarrass us. We didn't grow up thinking of ourselves as sexual beings, and perhaps that is good in a way since most human interactions—at work, at the store, on the bus, with friends, co-workers, and strangers—don't revolve around this aspect of ourselves. Maybe the Buddhists are right: desire increases suffering. People who seem driven to express their sexuality at all times are usually unhappy. I *am* thankful not to have been taught to hate my body out of guilt because sex is a sin—or out of a sense of inadequacy because my body isn't good enough to let me enjoy my sin.

But I don't think Japanese girls are truly lucky, either, to have a politely desexualized view of the body. In my mid-twenties, already living in Wisconsin, I was shocked to learn that sex was, in some ways, a big deal in Japan. I read an article about Japanese businessmen who go on "sex tours" to Thailand. The article said that the wives of these business-men fully understand the nature of the tours and even pack condoms in their husbands' suitcases. Around the same time, I met Americans who had studied in Japan and visited night-clubs where they saw strip shows and "live sex acts." They insisted that American pornographic movies are modest compared with the shows in Japan, which are easily accessi-ble to any man who is interested. The Japanese men who go on sex tours and visit live sex shows are ordinary middle-class and upper-middle-class businessmen—the kinds of men my Japanese friends have married.

I suppose I had been naive not to notice the erotic dimen-sion of Japanese culture. In high school, I had read parts of *The Tale of Genji,* which is a chronicle of the sexual adventures of a handsome court gentleman of the twelfth century. But I didn't think that the old novel had anything to do with my reality, any more than a typical freshman English student thinks *King Lear* has any bearing on his or her life. My art history books had a few reproductions of the *ukiyo-e* wood-block prints depicting courtesans in erotic poses. Again, I thought of those pictures the same way I thought of Michel-angelo's *David*—as something to discuss in an essay exam.

I did not realize that Japanese erotic culture had lasted into the present and was easily accessible to Japanese men. Nor did I know that the "nice" Japanese women, raised to regard themselves as nonsexual, had to pack condoms in their hus-bands' suitcases. I had been ironically right when I thought of sex as something that happened in a foreign country. I finally understood why many upper-middle-class Japanese women talk about their marriages in practical and businesslike ways, as though being a wife was a job or a position they had to hold. There is a division of labor among women. The job of a "nice" woman from an upper-middle-class family is to become a wife and a mother; another kind of woman—a woman from a poor family or a foreign woman—is exploited to perform the job of sexually satisfying men. Although sex is not completely synonymous with romance, love, or happiness, a marriage in which sex has nothing to do with romance, love, or happiness—merely to do with reproduction and health—can only be a business arrangement.

If marriage is like a job in Japan, it is a job that most Japanese women are desperate to get. For a Japanese woman, to be unmarried carries the same sort of stigma that being unemployed holds for Americans—especially for American men. People think that you are not contributing enough to society or making the right kind of progress through life: you are not fulfilling the role you were born for.

I am painfully aware of this stigma every time I go to Japan. During my last visit, I went to see an old high school friend, Hiroko. We had tea at her house and talked about other school friends.

"Did you know that Nobuko has gotten married?" Hiroko asked me.

I was surprised to hear the news. On a previous visit I had learned that Nobuko was regional manager for the Japanese branch of Hilton hotels. Always traveling to Europe on business, she loved her job and was perfectly content to live with her parents in their big house in Ashiya.

"About a year ago," Hiroko continued. "Nobuko decided to get married."

"To whom?" I asked, expecting to hear about some exotic and dramatic romance, possibly with a foreigner. (I already knew that Japanese men usually don't have big romances with the nice Japanese women they marry.)

"She had no one in mind," Hiroko said. "But she quit her job so she could put all her efforts into finding a suitable husband. She and her mother looked at stacks and stacks of résumés from older men looking for a wife."

Hiroko was saying that Nobuko had gone through an omiai, or marriage-arranging process: when someone is looking for a husband or a wife, her or his family consults other families to get the names of suitable people. Folders of information—résumés, photographs, birth certificates—are exchanged. Once a match is made, the families set up a group meeting at a public place like a restaurant or a hotel lobby. The man and the woman meet in the presence of their parents and even some of their siblings. If they like each other and the other members of the families have no objection, the couple begins to date so they can get to know each other a little before getting married. The marriage generally takes place within a few months.

"Nobuko and her mother didn't find anyone by asking their family friends, so they consulted an omiai-arranging service," Hiroko told me. "They must have looked at hundreds of résumés. They were looking for a well-to-do older man in Kobe or Osaka."

"What do you mean, older?" I asked. Nobuko would have been thirty-three at the time.

"Late forties, fifties, sixties," Hiroko explained. "There

aren't many men younger than forty-five who are widow-ers."

"But there must have been some men our age who were single because they'd never married," I pointed out.

"Sure, but those men have never been married because they have health problems, or they aren't the settling-down type, or their mothers are too domineering. Men like those don't make a lot of money, and they don't make good hus-bands. Nobuko and her mother were looking for reliable men who had been married once and then widowed. She didn't quit her job only to marry a playboy, a mommy's boy, or an invalid."

I picked up my teacup and tried to drink, but I felt sick. Hiroko made it sound as if our friend had to look for a job in a bad market.

"Anyway," Hiroko said, brightening, "Nobuko got lucky. She found a business executive of a trading company whose wife had passed away a couple of years ago. He was younger than most—in his late forties—and both of his kids were already in college, so she doesn't have to raise someone else's kids. It was by far the best situation."

"Have you met her husband?" I asked.

"No," Hiroko sighed. "My husband and I were still in Chicago when they got married. Soon afterward, Nobuko's husband got transferred to New York, so they moved there. I didn't get a chance to meet him or to say goodbye to Nobuko."

"Have you heard from her, though? Is she happy?" I asked.

Hiroko didn't answer right away, so I knew that meant some form of no.

"At least she'll get to use her English," I offered. I didn't know what else to say. Nobuko speaks English, German, and French, as well as Japanese.

"I know," Hiroko said. "That's one of the reasons the man wanted to marry her. Even when he was stationed in Osaka, he worked mostly with Americans and Europeans. Foreign businessmen like to socialize at people's homes. Being a widower was a real disadvantage to him. He wanted to marry someone who could carry on conversations with his guests, not just serve drinks and food and disappear into the kitchen. Nobuko was a good choice. She's smart. She can talk about anything."

I felt depressed to think of our friend quitting her job to become a multilingual hostess. "Why did she want to get married anyway?" I asked. That was the part I didn't understand: she had wanted to get married even though she had no one in mind. It wasn't as though she had met and fallen madly in love with someone and sacrificed her job to be with him. At least that would have made sense— she would have been driven by something compelling, if destructive. Although I would never choose reckless love that demands a big sacrifice, I understand its appeal for other people. That kind of love is like religion. Once you can accept the apparently irrational premise—that someone was crucified and then resurrected to atone for your sins, or that you and your lover were destined to be together and only he can make you happy—then everything else follows in an almost logical fashion. You can predict, accept, and even enjoy the consequences, the way skydivers must love the freefall that is the inevitable and desired consequence of their leap. Nobuko's actions were different.

Her choice seemed both calculated and reckless, for no good reason.

Hiroko didn't really answer my question. She just said, "Nobuko had to hurry because it was the last chance for her to be married. Time was running out."

"Why? You said that she was only looking to be a second wife to someone older. A second wife almost never has her own kids. She could have waited ten, fifteen years to be an old man's wife."

"Oh, come on," Hiroko said. "Nobody marries a woman over forty, even if he doesn't plan to have a child with her. Nobuko didn't have that much time."

I stared at my cup of cold tea, feeling suddenly too angry to speak. It was so unfair for a sixty-five-year-old man to say that a forty-one-year-old woman was "too old" to be his wife. *How can Hiroko accept this prejudice so easily?* I wondered. When I looked up, she shrugged her shoulders and made a sour face, a gesture of resignation. "All right," I said, trying to calm down and get back to my original question. "So let's say she was getting too old and didn't have much time. But I still don't understand. Why did she want to get married at all? I thought she was happy working for Hilton."

Hiroko shook her head. "It was a good job, I'm sure," she said. "But Nobuko worked so hard every day. All she did was work—even her travels were for work. That must have been such an empty feeling—to have nothing but your work."

It must be an empty feeling, equally, to be married to someone who wants a perfect wife to advance his career, but I could not point that out because that statement might apply to Hiroko, too. Hiroko had quit her job at an airline a few years back when her husband was chosen by his company to study for an M.B.A. in Chicago. To go with him and take care of him, she had to give up her job. He didn't speak much English. Hiroko is bilingual. He couldn't have lived in Chicago or done his homework in English without her help. Hiroko, too, was a perfect wife for her husband's career.

To be that perfect wife, she had given up a lot. Now that they were back in Japan, she was having a hard time finding a job: when she applied for jobs, she was told that she was qualified but too old. One employer even asked her if she had a friend with similar qualifications who was ten years younger. In Japan, where companies can openly discriminate against people on the basis of gender and age, Hiroko's chance of getting a good job didn't look great. Under those circumstances, she must want to believe, all the more, that marriage is more fulfilling than a job. It wasn't my place to contradict her and make her feel bad about herself and Nobuko. But I didn't think either of them was happy. Hiroko said nothing about her husband except that when they traveled together, they sometimes ran out of things to say to each other. That didn't sound promising at all. Hiroko was not an exception—all our friends from school talk in the same way about their husbands. They are intelligent and outspoken women, not at all the kind of people who expect little from life. Why do they put up with getting nothing from their husbands?

My friends and I—"nice" Japanese girls—had been taught that whatever we did for ourselves was "empty," while what we did to take care of other people, especially a husband or children, was "fulfilling." We grew up watching our mothers working hard as housekeepers, silent hostesses, and errand-women for our fathers, who never thanked their wives except by a begrudging nod or barely audible grunt.

We never saw our parents hug, never heard our fathers compliment our mothers on anything. Maybe we were too used to seeing our mothers making sacrifices for nothing. Women our age don't expect any more from their marriages than our mothers did.

In my generation, as well as in my mother's or grandmothers', Japanese marriages don't provide women with "happiness." None of my Japanese friends have ever talked about the great conversations they have with their husbands, the emotional support they get from them in times of trouble, or even the fun they have together on trips. People in Japan often say that the marriages of Americans—which are based on sexual attraction, love, and romance—can only lead to divorce because sexual attraction and love can fade away so easily. Japanese arranged marriages are more stable, they argue, since these matches are based on suitability. Maybe it's true that romance often brings together people who are not so compatible with each other—half of my American friends are divorced. But those who stay together do so by choice, trying to work out their differences because they love each other. I cannot imagine how a traditional Japanese couple starting out with nothing but "suitability" can feel the same motivation to be happy together when they turn out to be incompatible—which must happen to many couples since their "suitability" is based on family background, not personalities. I can only conclude that they stay together because stability is more important than the happiness of either party.

Whenever I talk to Japanese women, I wonder if personal happiness is an American concept. The concept of happiness as an emotional "high" or personal "fulfillment" seems foreign to my Japanese friends. To them, happiness means stability and family harmony, living day to day and feeling useful and valued rather than despised as a selfish person. Though all my friends come from upper-middle-class families, most Japanese women, regardless of class or education, seem to share the same sense of happiness-as-stability-and-hard-work-for-others. The only women who are allowed to have "fun" in a more American sense—doing things that aren't useful but enjoyable—are widows, women who have put in their time at the duty of marriage. These are women who are assumed to be too old for sex, love, or romance, and their "fun" usually involves spending time with old friends who are also widows. Finally free from men, these women can find happiness in one another's company.

A few days after I visited my friend Hiroko, I went to see Mrs. Kuzuha, a woman who had been a good friend of my mother's. Our two families had been neighbors in the early sixties, when we lived in the company-owned apartment complex before moving into houses of our own. Even after our move Mrs. Kuzuha and my mother spent a lot of time together; my brother and I played with the two Kuzuha boys, the younger of whom was my age. Until my mother's death, we were like an extended family with two mothers and four kids.

Mrs. Kuzuha made me dinner at her house up on a hill in Ashiya, where she lives alone. Her husband had died two years before from cancer. The boys had gotten married and moved to Kyoto and Tokyo.

"When my husband died," Mrs. Kuzuha told me at dinner, "I was sad, of course. He was a good person for the most part, though all men are selfish from time to time." She nodded in a discreet way and went on. "I don't resent him now for anything he did, and I was sorry for him during his illness. But it's good to be on my own now. I want to enjoy myself and be happy in my old age. I'm grateful to him for working so hard and leaving me comfortable."

She told me her daily routine. Every morning, she awoke at five and listened to the English conversation program on the radio. Lying in bed, she would repeat the sentences after the announcer. She wanted to improve her English because she and her friends often go to Europe on cruises. After getting up and having breakfast, she drove to the gym to exercise. She was in a Ping-Pong league.

"It isn't a league just for old people," she bragged, laughing. "There are men and women in their forties or even thirties. I have a pretty good serve. Once at a ski resort, I played with some college kids and won."

A few times a week, she also took karaoke-singing lessons. This was the first time I had ever even heard of lessons for karaoke.

"Oh, it's very popular," Mrs. Kuzuha said. "Singing is good for both the body and the spirit. It clears your head and makes you feel more cheerful. To sing, you have to stand up straight and take a deep breath. It's hard to feel depressed or lonely while standing up like that." She demonstrated by straightening her back.

We were having a typical Japanese dinner, at which the hostess gets up every few minutes to make more food. Mrs. Kuzuha had first prepared stir-fried vegetables and tofu. Halfway through that course, she got up to cook a Japanese-style omelette for me; then it was time to put together a green salad, to cut up some fruit, to make coffee, to offer me a slice of cheesecake. Offering food is how a Japanese woman shows her love. Mrs. Kuzuha was waiting on me as she had waited on her family all her life, while talking about how much she enjoyed being on her own.

"I only regret that your mother didn't live long enough to enjoy her old age," she told me. "Our husbands died within a year of each other. We could have been widows together. It would have been so nice to travel with her."

Being a Japanese widow is like being honorably retired. It is the only way a woman can be independent without being considered selfish.

I wasn't at all surprised to see Mrs. Kuzuha enjoying her new independence. I know some widowed women in the States who are very active and happy. In the last ten or fifteen years, many of my friends have lost one of their grandparents or parents. When someone's grandmother or mother died, the grandfather or the father often remarried right away or else got sick. When a woman was widowed, she tended to stay single. Though some suffered like the men, many became very independent. My friends' grandparents and parents came from the generation in which men's and women's duties were strictly divided. While the men were helpless around the house (cleaning, cooking, choosing the right things to wear), the women didn't know how to balance checkbooks, arrange for house repairs, or travel on their own. Some of my friends' mothers didn't know how to pump gas at self-service stations. About half the women continued to depend on their children and neighbors, but the other half began to relish their new responsibilities and skills. I admired these women and was happy to see that Mrs. Kuzuha was their Japanese counterpart.

As a typical Japanese housewife, Mrs. Kuzuha was much better prepared to be alone than the American women I know. Mrs. Kuzuha never relied on her husband to make decisions about cars and finances. More than that, she did not expect her husband to make her happy or give her a lot of companionship, so his absence does not leave a big hole in her life. Now that he is gone, she does not think, I wonder what my husband would have said about this? or I wish he could have seen that because he would have laughed. She can say in a dry and matter-of-fact tone, "My husband was a good man, but I am happy to be on my own to enjoy my life. I wish my best friend were still alive so we could have been widows together." I cannot imagine any American woman saying that.

Mrs. Kuzuha can be cheerful and matter-of-fact about her husband's death because she is a Japanese woman. Her frankness is not shocking to anyone around her; it's her widow's privilege. But her position in society is not the only reason for her independence. She told me that when she was in her early forties, my mother's death changed her life.

"I knew that your father was having an affair," she said, "because I was your mother's friend and she confided in me. But even my husband knew. He was in the office when someone said, 'Mr. Mori's wife just died.' Another man who was there said, 'Which wife?' " She paused and continued. "I was angry at my husband even though he wasn't the one who had made the comment. All those men. They bragged to each other about their mistresses; they made me sick. Your mother's death changed everything for me. When I saw her in the coffin—she was so smart and beautiful and this is how she ended up—I said to myself, 'No man is going to drive me to this. I have to be strong and never depend on any man.'" She shook her head and sighed.

"Back then, I had no choice but to depend on my husband," Mrs. Kuzuha continued. "I didn't have any skills. I couldn't make my own living. I had to stay home and raise our children. It wasn't as though I could leave him and be on my own or go back to live with my parents without embarrassing them. Until your mother's death, I had been resigned to all that. But my feelings changed. After your mother's death, I made a resolution. I decided to expect nothing from my husband from then on, even though I stayed married to him. I knew I had to be happy on my own."

When I visited Mrs. Kuzuha, I was already feeling unsure about my own marriage. After I got back to Green Bay, I often thought about my conversation with her. I kept remembering my mother's funeral—the large bouquets of yellow chrysanthemums, the white incense smoke, the black and white drapery signaling death. Surrounded by these colors of mourning, Mrs. Kuzuha and I had made the exact same resolution. Seeing my mother in the coffin, I, too, had said to myself: I will never depend on any man to make me happy, I will be happy on my own. I was twelve then. I planned never to marry.

Twenty-four years later, I was married to a perfectly nice man. We had promised to make each other happy. And yet when we started disagreeing about where to live or how to spend our time together, I couldn't try to work out our differences because I had never put aside my resolution from 1969. Even though I was married, I still considered myself to be on my own: I didn't want to give up anything for anyone else—nor did I expect anyone to give up anything for me. Married or single, I believed, all of us are basically on our own through life.

"Nothing against my husband personally," I often said to friends, "but I don't ever want my marriage to be the most important thing in my life. I would have been just as happy if I had never married him. My life would have been different but as good."

It was, I had to admit, an odd thing for a married person to say. I wondered if Chuck ever felt hurt to hear me say it. Many of the statements I made, I began to realize, must have sounded insensitive, even though I had only meant to be honest. When Chuck bought a motorcycle, I told him—and all my friends—that I was never going to ride on it because one of my childhood friends had died in a motorcycle accident and I had vowed never to drive or ride on one. When my friends asked me, "So how can you let your husband drive his motorcycle?" I answered, "I don't think it's my place to make decisions for him. He's an adult. He can make up his own mind. What he does is absolutely none of my business." What I said was fair—I expected to give and receive a lot of freedom—but in a way, I was saying that he was free to hurt himself or even die.

Once, Chuck asked me a question that surprised me. We were talking about his grandmother Alice, who had died of cancer two years after her husband's death. "I think my grandmother didn't want to be alive without my grandfather," he said. "She didn't want to be left all by herself.

What do you think? When we get old, do you feel like it's better to die first or to be left alone?"

"That's kind of a morbid thing to ask, isn't it?" I asked.

"It's just a theoretical question. What do you think?"

"Is this a trick question?" I began to laugh because the whole thing seemed absurd.

"It's not a trick question," he insisted.

"If I don't die first, my health is going to be OK and I'm going to have enough money to retire on and all that, right? Being left alone doesn't mean being sick or poor."

"That's right," he said.

By this time, I was laughing so hard that I could scarcely answer. I managed to say, "Of course I don't want to die first. If I'm going to be healthy and have enough money, why would I want to die rather than be a widow?"

"What about because you would miss me and you wouldn't want to be alone?"

"You must be kidding," I said. "Sure I'd miss you, but not enough to want to shorten my own life. I hope you'd feel the same way yourself."

He was quiet and he wouldn't look at my face, so I knew he was offended. Even then, I thought it was because I had unintentionally insulted his grandmother. "Listen, I wasn't saying that your grandmother was a weak person or anything like that," I offered. "She came from a different generation. I understand why she felt she didn't want to live without her husband. But we are different. We have no reason to be dependent on each other." Chuck just shrugged, so I thought he was telling me that he'd accepted my explanation. We started talking about something else.

I now understand why Chuck felt hurt. He was saddened by my refusal to love him in a traditional way. Chuck is not a dependent or needy person at all. But even he believed in conventional romance and love—men and women wanting to die together rather than lose each other. It hurt him that I dismissed this ideal as irrational and even pathetic.

If I had been more thoughtful, I would not have sounded so insulting. I don't think the romantic ideal of eternal love is pathetic. I shouldn't have laughed when Chuck seemed to be advocating it. But I still would have told him that romantic and eternal love is like a religion I cannot believe in. When I meet someone who is deeply religious or in love, I can see why people have always talked of devotion as a kind of light: men and women with strong faith or love have eyes that shine or faces that look radiant. I can admire the beauty of their ideal from a distance, but it isn't for me. Wanting to die for love strikes me as an irrational wish.

Maybe this is my legacy from Japan: I can be only as practical about love as I am about the body. Even though I did not want a Japanese marriage, which I consider oppressive, I never trusted the American ideal of romance and love that is forever. What I wanted was something different from both of these traditions, something more practical but also fair.

If marriage can be compared to a car trip, a traditional Japanese marriage is a journey in which all the destinations as well as the routes are decided by society. The couple is handed a detailed itinerary they must follow. The man provides the car, the food, all the necessary supplies. Having done that, he can sit in the passenger's seat and sleep, never saying a word. It is the woman who navigates and drives all the way in every kind of weather. No matter how tired she is, she can never ask the man to take over and let her rest; she just keeps driving, scarcely stopping to sleep or eat. This trip, obviously, would not be "fun." I can't imagine why any woman would want to get into the car except that standing on the side of the road, without a car, gives her a deep sense of shame and fear. She would rather be inside a car, where she can believe that she is secure.

In an ideal American marriage, the man and the woman jointly decide where they want to go, how to get there, and what to do along the way. They share the expenses and the driving and have fun together, but if they disagree about where to go or what to do, one of them will have to give up something he or she wants. If the trip works out, both parties are happy even though neither got everything he or she wanted. This is a trip I can understand as being worthwhile and good, though not for me.

The marriage I wanted—and had with Chuck for thirteen years—was one in which both the man and the woman had his or her own car. We would still travel in the same direction and stop along the way to meet—to share our experiences, to have fun, and to decide where to get together again. So long as we made it to our meeting place at the agreed-upon time, each of us was free to pick his or her own route and to do what he or she wanted. This marriage worked for us, but it didn't prepare us for the time when we began to have serious disagreements about the direction each of us wanted to travel. The only logical solution was simply to go our separate ways, which we were prepared to do since both of us were used to being on our own. That isn't to say that we do not miss each other's company or the familiar routine of meeting along the way to share our stories. Splitting up was hard. It was sad. But it wasn't anything like dying or wanting to die.

I don't trust love or romance because my mother married for love, only to discover that my father did not return her love in the same way. When he started having affairs a few years into their marriage, my mother must have regretted not having married the nice family friend her parents had wanted her to marry. In the end, my mother died for love even though her dying took seventeen years instead of one dramatic moment. But if I hadn't experienced this family tragedy, or if I hadn't grown up in Japan, I still would not have imagined a straight and smooth path in romance. It isn't easy for a woman my age, in America, to take love and marriage for granted. Most of my women friends in the Midwest have—or had—the marriage of two cars, and many are divorced. "I don't want to depend on some guy to make me happy," my friend Deb says. "I'd rather go out with a bunch of friends than be on a date with a guy who's opening doors for me and trying to help me put on my coat and hovering over me."

Even my friend Diane, who is married and happy, says that marriage is difficult because it comes with so much cultural and personal baggage. Our women friends—American, educated, and feminist—have a hard time making traditional gestures of love to their husbands or boyfriends. We hesitate to cook a nice dinner, dress in a traditionally "attractive" way, or wash our partner's clothes because these are the things women do in relationships where they are inferior to men. Most of us lived with other women before our marriages and were perfectly willing to cook a special dinner for our roommates; if our roommates left clothes in the washer, we didn't think twice about sorting them out to dry before washing our own clothes. We didn't show the same consideration to our husbands. When they left clothes in the washer, we moved them into the laundry basket, so we could load ours. "You left some clothes in the washer," we pointed out politely but coldly.

My friends and I are exceptions. The majority of American women take on the bulk of the household and child-care duties. But that made it worse for us. Every time Diane, our friends, and I saw how much other women put up with, we felt even less willing to be "nice" to our husbands. Maybe it was unfair of us to blame our husbands for other people's sexism, but that's what we did. Seeing other women make so many sacrifices, we vowed to ourselves that we would make none.

Once I started going to Japan every couple of years, I had even more "baggage" about marriage. I was appalled when my Japanese friends said that their husbands were so "understanding" because they didn't demand dinner the moment they returned from work. "He is so patient," my friends said. "When I've been very busy all day" (taking care of the kids or nursing his sick father or working part time) "my husband offers to go eat at a corner restaurant so I can just get the kids fed and make something easy for myself. He lets me not have to worry about him." I felt furious when I heard these comments. I couldn't believe that the best the men could do was to excuse their wives from taking care of them. Why can't these men make a caring gesture themselves, I wondered. Most Japanese cities have delis and pizza parlors. It wouldn't be difficult at all for any man to offer to go and get food for his whole family when his wife is busy or tired. I was angry that my friends' husbands never performed any simple acts of kindness, and I was irritated with my friends for expecting so little. If, a week later at home, I found a shirt Chuck had left in the washer, I took it out and set it on top of the dryer without even smoothing it out. I wasn't going to take care of his dirty laundry.

Sometimes, when I think of marriages, bodies, or sexuality, I get a hopeless feeling. Everybody is confused, it seems; there is no happy medium for women in dealing with these issues. We hate our bodies or we politely deny the body's sexuality. We resign ourselves to too much compromise or rebel against any compromise. Knowing two cultures only makes me more angry rather than giving me helpful insights.

I was comforted, then, to spend a week at a craft school last summer with a dozen other women from Wisconsin, Illinois, and Indiana. We were taking a weeklong class about using beads to make jewelry and to embellish garments. The school was on an island in northeastern Wisconsin: it consisted of three barns converted into studio spaces and a dorm. We sewed and strung beads all day and then slept in a big room that had twelve bunk beds. Most of the women were in their forties, fifties, or sixties—all but two were married and had children. For all of us, "beading" was a hobby, not a way to make money; we were reasonably comfortable but not wealthy—we worked as high school or college teachers, psychologists, social workers, nurses, or homemakers. We had never met one another before, but by the end of the week, after sitting at the long tables beading together, going out to eat at night at a local restaurant, and sharing the small living space, we had gotten to know one another pretty well.

Almost every night the married women called their husbands and children to make sure they were all right. A few of
them said that before leaving home they had spent a couple
of days baking pies and casseroles, then labeling and freezing
them because their husbands and children didn't know how
to cook. One woman had a mother-in-law with a resort cottage on the island. Her husband and son were coming up to
spend two days in the cottage while she was taking the class.
The day before they arrived, the woman said, "I'm worried
what the two of them will be wearing tomorrow. My husband doesn't know how to match the right shirt with the
right pair of pants. He would wear plaids and stripes together, and my son's not much better." Every day at home
she cooked everyone's meal and told everyone which shirt
matched which pants.

These episodes about inept husbands and dependent children didn't make me feel angry, as they usually did. The
women in my class had overcome their concerns or guilty
feelings and given themselves a whole week to do something
useless and enjoyable. Even as hobbies go, beadwork—unlike
weaving rugs or knitting sweaters—is impractical, not at all
beneficial to husbands and children. What we made—bead-
embroidered jackets, earrings, and woven necklaces—could
be worn only by ourselves and other women. My classmates
were doing something purely for themselves. If they had to
spend a few days beforehand baking casseroles so they could
get away, that was fine by them.

The woman whose husband and son visited for two days
said after they left, "I'm kind of relieved that they're gone.
When they were around, I had a hard time concentrating on
class because I felt like I should spend more time with
them." I loved her admitting that to me, nearly a stranger.

What I experienced that week would never happen in Japan. My Japanese friends would not feel entitled to leave their families for a week to pursue a hobby. I felt sad for them, but I was happy to have an opportunity I would never have had if I hadn't left home.

One night in the middle of that week, I woke up around three and sat up in my bunk bed by the window. I could hear the other eleven women snoring in their beds. Nobody was snoring very loudly. As I told them the next morning, it wasn't a snoring solo but a chorus, everyone doing her part and blending into the general noise. I wasn't bothered by it at all. I lay back down and was happy to close my eyes and go back to sleep. I was sure that I, too, would be snoring soon. I was comforted by the presence of these sleeping women—their bodies, their minds, their soft snoring. We were learning something together.

SYMBOLS

My cousin Kazumi once told me that the big difference between Dutch-style flower arrangement and the traditional Japanese *ikebana* is in the use of colors.

"When I took my first class from a Dutch teacher in Osaka," she said, "I had to learn about colors. There were ten people in my class—all of us had studied *ikebana*. Our teacher spent the first two weeks on color theory. He taught the class like an art class, and my classmates and I were slow to catch on. We had never been taught about the color wheel or the complementary colors."

"Colors aren't important in *ikebana*?" I asked.

"Not really," Kazumi replied. "Both in *ikebana* and in everyday arrangements, Japanese people always use the same colors. You'll notice if you go to any flower shop in town. Every bouquet has yellow, pink, and white. That's the most popular color combination in Japan. My Dutch teacher hated

those colors together. Any time one of us made an arrangement with them, he groaned and asked us to take it apart and
start over."

Ever since we've had this conversation, I automatically
scan the displays of ready-made bouquets at Japanese flower
shops. Kazumi was right. Almost every arrangement consists
of yellow, pink, and white: yellow mums, pink carnations,
white daisies; yellow lilies, pink roses, white tulips; yellow
roses, pink gerbera, white lilies of the valley. The combinations are endless but the colors remain the same. Bouquets at
upscale flower shops sometimes have a fourth color added as
a variation, but if they do, it's always a pale blue—a few
delphiniums or bachelor's buttons.

Kazumi didn't know how this yellow-pink-white color
tradition started or why it has endured. The three colors, she
and I agree, don't look very good together. I don't think we
are unfairly applying Western aesthetic principles to Japanese
flowers. There is something universal about color theory,
about the way the human eye responds to light and shade.
No matter what culture we come from, our eyes are drawn
to the high contrast of complementary colors or the soothing
gradations of similar colors. There are color combinations—
usually from non-Western cultures—that defy the traditional
understanding of the color wheel: the bright pink and the
leaf green of Hmong embroidery or the turquoise blue and
the dark orange of Native American jewelry. But these colors
come from natural surroundings: every bright pink flower
has green leaves and stems; out in the canyon country, the
blue sky and the rust-orange rock face is the most noticeable
color juxtaposition. The yellow-pink-white combination is
seldom seen together in nature. In Japan as well as in most

temperate climates, the pink and purple wildflowers of early spring are over long before the yellow flowers, like sunflowers, black-eyed Susans, and milkweed, bloom in midsummer.

The only way I can understand the yellow-pink-white palette is to interpret it as a code. A Japanese bouquet is a symbol composed of all the right meanings: yellow signifies "cheerful and bright," pink is for "pretty," white is an auspicious color of harmony, and the green leaves indicate "prosperity." Pale blue connotes subtle good taste or refinement, so it's added to expensive bouquets. Together, the flowers have all the right meanings, and nothing is added that does not contribute to the overall symbolic representation of "beauty" and "auspicious wishes."

Everyday life in Japan is full of visual and auditory symbols that a person can understand only by decoding the message, symbol by symbol, in the way I have come to understand the colors of the flowers. When I lived in Japan as a child and a teenager, I had no clue about how to understand the traditional culture of my own country. Japanese literature, music, and art baffled me because I did not yet know that the Japanese concept of beauty—in art or in everyday life—relies on a strict adherence to an impersonal code of symbols: a beautiful object must be harmonious and smooth, having all the right symbolic elements and containing no surprises. My "Americanized" education prepared me to approach art as a personal expression—to notice the small but genuine surprises that reveal distinct individual styles and voices. Trying to view Japanese art, which offered no surprises or revelations, I did not know what I was supposed to be looking for.

Now I know that I am supposed to notice the symbols and

appreciate the meticulous care people have taken to present the right symbol at the right time. I understand why all my women friends in Japan dress in the same way and speak with the same voice. Every Japanese woman is expected to pay strict attention to detail, whether she is practicing tea ceremony or wrapping her friend's birthday gift, so that the way she holds the teacup or the ribbon she chooses for the wrapping will be just the right thing—that is to say, the exact same thing everyone else would choose. Uniformity is the key to beauty and decorum. That's why all Japanese stores, at closing every day, play "Auld Lang Syne" over their P.A. systems. The tune is a symbol of closing time; no other music can be played at that time. In Japanese restaurants, fruit salad is always served on a bed of bibb or Boston lettuce, on a clear glass plate.

These practices only make sense as symbols. No one is expected to eat the lettuce with the banana or the peach in the "beautifully" served fruit salad. The green lettuce symbolizes "refreshing," as does the glass plate. The lettuce is different from the ubiquitous sprig of parsley used as a garnish at American restaurants. Though few people actually eat the parsley, it goes with dishes where they might. In Japan, parsley and nothing else (like mint, which might taste better with fruit) can decorate plates of fruit salads or "fruit sandwiches"—sandwiches with finely chopped fruit salad as a filling. Those sandwiches, too, can only be explained as symbols: sandwiches mean "light and refreshing meal," so fruit salad is as good a filling as sliced cucumbers.

There are peculiar combinations of food in any culture. I don't look forward to potluck dinners in the Midwest because I feel obligated to try strange foods like Jell-O salad. In

Green Bay, you can't go to a neighborhood picnic or a family-reunion potluck-in-the-park and not see a pan of lime Jell-O with shredded carrots, or orange Jell-O with finely chopped celery. There seems to be a strict sense of tradition about the combination: it is important to have the orange and the green together—the orange Jell-O never has carrots, and the lime Jell-O never has celery. I used to think that I didn't like these Jell-O salads because they were weird American foods I hadn't grown up with. Although my family ate mostly "Western" meals (toast and eggs for breakfast, sandwiches for lunch, casseroles for dinner), we certainly did not have "traditional" specialties like Jell-O salads or Waldorf salad, another dish I try to avoid at picnics.

Maybe I don't like these salads because they are American versions of the yellow-pink-white flowers: they are results of "tradition" overriding what would naturally appeal to the eye or the taste buds. "Tradition" is the only explanation for the combination of walnuts, raisins, celery, apples, and mayonnaise. The salad was originally served at New York's Waldorf-Astoria Hotel at the turn of the century by the maitre d' who also invented chicken Diane and veal Oscar. I am not sure why this particular salad, of all the hundreds of recipes that must have been served at the Waldorf-Astoria, has become the mainstay of Midwestern family get-togethers and banquets, but it has. The version served at my college has miniature marshmallows in it.

The difference between the American food tradition and the Japanese, though, is that most Americans don't revere Jell-O and Waldorf salads as models of ultimate fine taste. A lot of my friends make fun of their Aunt Martha's Jell-O salad, which they eat out of politeness; they don't like walnuts or raisins in oatmeal cookies, much less in salads. American strange food combinations are old-fashioned recipes for my friends to laugh about or feel nostalgic about because they mean childhood, home, family, and holiday get-togethers. These dishes are personal or family symbols of tradition or good times for some people, but they are not part of the oppressive code of what is universally considered to be fine taste. In Japan, there is no such thing as a personal or family symbol: all symbols are universal, and adhering to them is how everyone tries to show good breeding. Lettuce is served with fruit salad in expensive restaurants, "Auld Lang Syne" is played at upscale department stores, and yellow-pink-white bouquets are tied with silk ribbons behind immaculately polished glass. I have no problem with bad taste that is homey. I am much less comfortable with the exaltation of bad taste into symbols of correct form that everyone must follow.

Although I did not fully understand the importance of everyday symbolism until I was an adult, I always noticed the way people in Japan fell into uncomfortable silence when they saw someone dressed in the wrong color. Even as children, we were taught that boys must never wear pink or red, and that we should not sit next to a man in a purple or yellow shirt on the train because he is probably a *yakuza* or a foreigner. There were rules about what colors everyone should wear according to their age and gender, and people who did not obey these rules were sure to be up to no good.

When I came to America, I was relieved that the rules about colors were much more relaxed. Americans tend to dress their boy babies in powder blue and their girl babies in pale pink, but some people shun this practice as sexist. American business executives prefer navy blue and avoid colors that are regarded as frivolous, not fit for business attire: certain shades of pink, lavender, or red, colors traditionally associated with femininity. But the hockey coach at our college wears a pale pink cardigan now and then, and my friend Fred buys women's singlets and shorts for running because he looks bad in the dark colors marketed for men. No one labels the hockey coach or Fred as suspicious characters or considers them to be eccentric. In Japan, to appear in the "wrong" color just once is to be branded as someone who doesn't know or care what is right and proper.

The color rules are fairly easy for Japanese men. All they have to do is avoid reds and pinks as young boys and then settle into a wardrobe of navy, black, and white when they grow up to be businessmen. Women have more choices, but in Japan, having choices usually means having more ways to go wrong.

As soon as I was old enough to learn the names of colors in kindergarten, I became aware that there were old-woman colors and young-woman colors, as well as boy colors and girl colors. The differences between old-woman colors and young-woman colors seemed much more complicated than those between boy colors and girl colors. From the way my mother complained about her mother's clothes, I could see that they didn't agree about how strictly my grandmother should follow the rules.

"Your grandmother dresses too much like an old woman," my mother often said when we went shopping. "I would love to buy that dark green wool and knit her a sweater, but she'll never wear it. She only likes clothes that are very jimi."

Jimi means, literally, "earth-taste," though it does not refer to what Westerners think of as earth tones. The word is used to refer to colors that are subdued: dark gray, dark brown, navy blue. As far back as I can remember, Fuku wore these colors exclusively, in house dresses and blouse-skirt combinations that were large and shapeless. The only "good" clothes she had were the formal black kimonos with the family crest embroidered in white. She wore the kimonos only to weddings or funerals. My mother, who wanted her mother to look a little "more modern," would send her dresses she had sewn herself. The dresses were by no means bright or flashy: modest cotton or wool A-lines in silver-gray, cobalt blue, or maybe maroon if my mother was feeling hopeful that Fuku would change.

Maroon was as daring as an old woman could dress. My mother was careful not to send anything inappropriate; still, the new clothes stayed in Fuku's dresser drawers. They were too beautiful to wear, Fuku insisted. Every time we visited, my mother was depressed to see the clothes neatly folded and stored, never worn.

The old-woman colors looked and sounded depressing to me. In Japanese, even their names are dismal. Nezumi-iro (mouse color) for dark gray; cha-iro (tea color) for dark brown; hai-iro (ash color) for white-gray. The names reminded me of bleak farm kitchens. Sooner or later, everyone obeyed the rules and resigned themselves to these dismal-sounding colors. Even my mother complied when it came to her turn. In her mid-thirties, she gave away several of her dresses and suits to her younger sister and sisters-in-law, saying they were now too *hade* ("stick-out" and "flashy")—the opposite of jimi—for her. The clothes she gave away weren't in colors I now think of as bright. By the time my mother was my mother, she no longer wore bright pinks, reds, or yellows, the colors of childhood and youth. When she became thirty-five, even light blue (which has a beautiful name in Japanese: mizu-iro, "water color") and forest green (midori, another pretty-sounding name, sometimes used as a woman's name) were too *hade*. She was supposed to move on to the browns and dark blues, and in ten years, she would have to give up even these colors and wear only the grays and the darkest blues.

My mother was forty-one when she killed herself. She never completed her transition into the brown-and-dark-blue middle age. She was a woman who spent her weekends viewing the Impressionists, who stayed up past midnight embroidering pink flowers and delicate yellow butterflies on my blouses. In her dresser drawers, she left boxes of embroidery floss, in colors she could no longer wear. A month after her death, I began seventh grade at a private girls' school—the only junior high school in the Kobe-Osaka area that didn't require uniforms. For the first-day ceremony at the school, I wore a red dress my mother had made for me.

The color rules in Japan have not changed. On trains or buses, I still see older women in shapeless navy blue or dark gray dresses, young working women in pastel-colored suits, and, most noticeable of all, school-age girls in their somber-looking uniforms.

In Japan, colors signify not only age but also occasion and

attitude. The dark colors—black, navy blue, gray, dark brown—are worn to funerals, Buddhist ceremonies, and other formal events. These colors signal solemn feelings and serious purposes in general, not just grief or mourning. For that reason, they are used in school uniforms to set a solemn tone and to encourage a serious attitude—with the result that, at school, junior and senior high school students wear the same colors as old women.

All boys' and girls' school clothes are modeled after military uniforms: stiff and heavy fabrics, brass buttons, tight necks, squared shoulders. Both boys and girls must wear their uniforms to school and even on weekends if they go out alone or with other students. Boys' uniforms are black, while girls' uniforms are in the other "serious" colors such as navy blue, dark brown, dark gray. I don't think this is simply coincidence. In Japanese color symbolism, black is the most formal color—the color of mourning, but also the color of authority and decorum. It is stark and important. In judo or karate, black connotes highest achievement. While boys wear this important color to express their seriousness about studying, girls—just like old women—wear the less-powerful darker colors that are subdued and humble. Boys are taught to pursue knowledge as aggressively as they would train to earn black belts; girls and old women are encouraged to be serious but not stick out or call attention to themselves.

Subdued dark colors are not flattering to the young girls and the old women who must wear them. Stark colors like black and white set off some features, but muddy browns and ashy grays dull almost everyone's looks. It is no coincidence that these are the colors of "grunge" fashion: they look good only on people who appear very striking and a little off-center—a young woman with an asymmetrical hair-cut, theatrical make-up, and nose or eyebrow rings. School-age girls whose features and personalities are still unformed and old women who have had years of practice at not "stick-ing out" are the last people to benefit from colors that are called mouse and tea.

Riding the trains or buses in Japan, I also notice a peculiar reversal. While teenage girls are required to wear "sailor dresses" and thick blazers in somber colors, young women in their twenties who no longer have to wear uniforms—except when going to work in tailored suits—choose frilly, childlike fashions: ribbons, bows, laces, full skirts. These clothes resemble young girls' party dresses in style if not in color. The ribboned and bowed style goes with the high squeaky voice a well-bred young woman is expected to use in public. A young Japanese woman is trained to look and sound like a child. That, too, is a symbol—a symbol of inno-cence and cuteness.

The childish look of a twenty-eight-year-old Japanese woman is completely different from the MTV teenager mode some American women affect well into their twenties or thirties. One is a denial of sexuality, while the other is an attempt to communicate a youthful and daring eroticism. These styles are reflections of each culture's fantasies about women. In Japan, an ideal woman is a quiet wife who serves her man with childlike obedience and innocence. American popular culture encourages women to be young temptresses, eager to satisfy men sexually but having no grown-up ideas or demands. In both fantasies, an attractive woman is a woman whose growth is stunted.

In any culture women's clothes and makeup are full of

what my friend Diane calls "sexist baggage." That baggage adds to the insecurity most of us feel about our appearance. I've often wondered why I feel insecure about looking good when I know that I am not and will never be beautiful. With everything else, insecurity goes hand in hand with the possibility of doing well. I feel insecure about giving a lecture, writing a book, or planning a party because these are things I *can* do well and not doing so will be a disappointment. I dread giving a newspaper interview or showing important guests around town, but I don't feel *insecure* about these occasions: I don't wonder how I sounded in the interview or if I was a good guide, since I already know that I sounded stupid and got lost while driving the guests around. I don't expect to look good, any more than I expect to sound intelligent in interviews, and yet I often feel insecure: I worry if my sweater looks too "dorky," if my ears are sticking out in a funny way, if I am making the wrong impression.

Personal appearance causes anxiety and insecurity because even those of us who are not beautiful consider our clothes, makeup, or hair style to be expressions or symbols of who we are, and yet our choices are burdened by cultural, societal, and sexist expectations. Personal appearance is the four-way intersection where our personal symbolism clashes with the symbolism of the culture in which we must live. For some of us, it's a head-on collision, a big highway catastrophe.

The consolation of living in America is that if I am careful, I can navigate my way through this dangerous intersection, avoiding the cultural and sexist expectations that come barreling down like a semi. I can devise my own system of determining what is acceptable or unacceptable for my own standard of gender equality. I can avoid "fashion" items—like pantyhose or high heels—that seem designed to torture a woman's body and have no counterpart in male attire. I don't wear rouge, eye makeup, lipstick, or foundation, since my male colleagues are not required to improve their appearances in a similar fashion. But if I choose to wear batik shirts, beaded jewelry, or long hair, I can reason that I am not drawn to that style because I am a woman: were I a man, I would be a middle-aged hippie guy with a ponytail and a beaded necklace, as some of my male friends are. Even in a small town in the Midwest, it is possible for me to express my personality, avoid the stereotypes I abhor, and still present an appearance that does not label me as an offensive or eccentric person.

In Japan, nobody can negotiate a similar peace. Every woman wears the same makeup unless she wants to be an outcast. The last time I stayed at my aunt's and cousin's house, I got up one morning to see Kazumi putting on her makeup at the kitchen table. She had already applied a thick, smooth foundation and was now painting her lips in dark red—first outlining the shape of her lips and then carefully filling in the rest. When she was done, she had the same face every "nice" Japanese woman wears: thick foundation and lipstick, but no rouge, eye shadow, or mascara. She reminded me of the young Japanese women I see at American airports—before they utter a word, I can tell that they are Japanese, not Chinese or Korean, because of this makeup.

It was unsettling to see my own cousin in the makeup that makes every woman look the same. Nice-Japanese-woman makeup is so obviously a mask or a symbol of calm femininity. The foundation and the lipstick emphasize a smooth surface—a peaceful and flawless face, a tightly closed mouth. The more aggressive or expressive parts of a woman's face— the eyes, the cheekbones—are hidden or almost erased. A Japanese woman is considered beautiful for having a pure, empty face.

The difference between my cousin's situation and mine is not that the makeup she is supposed to wear is worse than the one that is most available to me. The popular makeup of an American woman—wide-open eyes, red lips, sharply de-lineated cheekbones—gives her a constantly surprised and vulnerable appearance as though she were an old-fashioned heroine in need of rescue. But if I do not wear that makeup, I am not subjected to a harsh judgment. Most people I see day-to-day don't even notice whether I am wearing makeup, much less care.

In Japan, everyone notices—even on the rare occasion when they decide not to pass judgment. If I don't wear the nice-woman makeup on my visits, people are not offended: I am almost a foreigner, so I am allowed to be different. But everyone comments on it all the same, using the word that means "not wearing makeup" (*sugao* or "original face"): "I notice you are always going about *sugao*," they say. My free-dom may be a freedom from judgment, but not from inter-pretation. Now that I am a foreigner, a person who "rejected" Japan, everything I do is interpreted as a symbol of my nonconformist philosophy. "Oh, you don't wear makeup and you are a vegetarian," I am told. "That's be-cause you are a person who values the simple life. You de-spise false appearances, and you believe in not harming nature." When I try to explain that my choices have more to do with personal preferences than big moral philosophies, people smile indulgently as though I were only trying to be polite or modest. "Oh, I understand," they say. "A person like you, who likes the simple life and nature, never brags."

In Japan, there is no such thing as a purely personal choice. Everything you do (or decide not to do) is a symbolic message directed at the world, a manifesto of a philosophical cause you support. Even your rebellion, then, will be interpreted as a sign of your belonging to another group. You don't have to worry about the clash of personal symbolism and larger, cultural symbolism. Either your personal symbolism is the same as everyone's, or else you can ride in one of the few symbolic vehicles marked for outsiders and rejects.

When I studied Japanese poetry as an adult, I realized that Japanese literature—just like Japanese life in general—is a complicated system of symbols that few outsiders can understand. In 1983, in one of my preliminary projects for my doctorate, I set out to translate the poems of eleven Japanese women—most of them born in the 1920s and 1930s. They were contemporaries of my mother and also of the American women poets I admire: Maxine Kumin, Sylvia Plath, Anne Sexton. I was not familiar with the works of contemporary Japanese women, so I had high hopes of discovering some new favorites. But in the end, I was disappointed by the poems I tried to translate.

Though many of the poems were very personal and perhaps even confessional in feeling—distraught with anger, loneliness, or frustrated ambition—they struck me as disturbingly abstract in expression. Some of the poems ended in

clichés and slogans about how women must realize that working in a kitchen is a service to a higher art, or how nature can
refresh the mind. The others—a majority—looked more interesting but baffled me because they belonged to the other
extreme: the poets used disjointed and abstract images no one
could possibly understand—spinning umbrellas falling from
the sky, riderless carriages speeding down deserted streets at
high noon, glass-encased rooms floating among clouds.
Though these images evoked powerful anxiety and unhappiness, I could not understand how they were connected: how
did those spinning umbrellas lead, two stanzas later, to the
glass-encased rooms, and what does this all mean? The Japanese women were writing in the two extreme ways that I ask
my students to avoid—spouting off predictable philosophy or
using language as a *code* and constructing poems that are word
puzzles no one can understand.

The Japanese poets were writing in their native tradition,
which has always relied on big themes and symbolism. I
could see the similarity between their work and the traditional haiku that my friends and I studied in high school.
Every haiku has a coded reference to one of the seasons:
snow, brown leaves (winter); violets, cherries (spring);
frogs, morning glories (summer); eggplant, chrysanthemums (autumn). A haiku can say so much in seventeen sylla-
bles because every Japanese reader is trained to understand
these seasonal references, to know that every seemingly casual observation about frogs jumping into ponds is a symbolic comment about an elusive summer moment and,
ultimately, the transient nature of life (which is the big
theme of every haiku in one way or another).

The difference between Basho—the best-known haiku

poet—and the twentieth-century women poets is that the women could no longer rely on a ready-made and universally agreed-upon system of symbols. The women, who wanted to write about twentieth-century feelings of anxiety and frustration, were left to create a highly personalized and enigmatic system of symbols and dream visions instead of coming back to those frogs and violets. But, having rejected the universal symbolism, they could only create personal symbols that were so eccentric that no one else could understand them. The paradox of contemporary American literature is that the more specific and detailed the writing is, the more powerful and rich its potential impact: the genuinely individual voice can also be universally appealing. In Japan, where everyone expects to understand each other without trying hard and so much reverence is paid to shared truths, the universal emotions the women poets wanted to write about—anger, frustration, sorrow—somehow misfired in their personal expressions.

The Japanese women poets seemed hurt more than helped by the tradition they had to draw on; the legacy of big ideas and nature symbols didn't offer them anything to adapt to their advantage. Reading their work added to the frustration I always felt about the haiku. Haiku poems are deceptive. Many Americans consider them charmingly simple because they seem to evoke everyday events in the forms of nature-inspired observations. In truth, haiku are not about nature. The moment a haiku poet hears or sees an actual object of nature, that object is transformed into a symbol. Basho does not think of his frog as an actual and particular frog in the way Maxine Kumin begins her poem "The Retrieval System" with an actual and particular dog:

> It begins with my dog, now dead, who all his long life
> carried about in his head the brown eyes of my father,
> keen, loving, accepting, sorrowful, whatever;
> they were Daddy's all right, handed on, except
> for their phosphorescent gleam tunneling the night
> which I have to concede was a separate gift.

Basho's frog is simply a switch that turns on the light of profound meaning. Although the dog causes Kumin to ponder the nature of loss and redemption and hope, the reader never forgets that this dog is a particular dog with particular brown eyes.

As teenagers, my friends and I did not want to hear or write about the transitory nature of life in general. We wanted to talk about ourselves—our real lives with friends, dogs and cats, parents. Most of us kept diaries, and those of us who read were drawn to the poetry of American women. It's hard to grow up in a place where nothing is allowed to be personal: in adolescence, everything is personal, even if you live in a culture that says otherwise.

Now that I am an adult, I understand why many of my American friends are attracted to haiku and Zen meditation, why they love the Japanese culture of symbolism in which everything reflects big universal values. My American friends "found" Eastern philosophy, art, religion, and literature during college. By then, they were tired of their own and their friends' personal anxieties, grievances, and high-strung neurotic behavior. Eastern culture gave my friends a chance to escape the personal, which they saw as petty obsession doomed to dead-end in some form of unhappiness. At twenty or twenty-one, my friends must have been disgusted

with their peers' lack of interest in the larger issues that af-
fected the world. In America, tolerance for individual differences can degenerate into plain and lame indifference. Every
time I hear my students dismiss people's ideas as "Well,
that's just their personal opinion," I understand how frustrated my friends must have been when they heard the same
comments at twenty. My friends—most of them very serious
and conscientious people—wanted to have universal ideas
that weren't dismissed as a personal whim or eccentricity.
When they discovered Zen and haiku in college, they must
have felt the same relief and joy I experienced the first time I
read Sylvia Plath and Anne Sexton and found out that it was
possible for a woman to express her anger by comparing her
father to a Nazi and a vampire or declaring that even God has
let her down.

Universal agreement is the key to Japanese conversations as
well as to haiku. Almost all platitudes mean the same thing in
Japan: the need to talk about something else. It matters very
little which platitude you choose, what its literal meaning is.
Once, to end a particularly depressing discussion among my
aunt, my brother, and me about what a bad father my father
was, my cousin Kazumi said, "Well, everyone has faults.
Faults and regrets—they are a big part of everyone's life."
While making this pessimistic pronouncement, she smiled
cheerfully and nodded to each one of us.

"That's true," I had to reply, trying to come up with
another platitude. "We all regret something in our lives."
That wasn't at all what I felt. I had nothing to regret just
then. It was my father who was a bad father, not me. I felt

self-righteous, which is the opposite of regretful. I was really saying to Kazumi, *Don't worry. I'm not as depressed as you think I am, but sure, we can talk about something else now.*

There was no way I could say that to her directly; nor was there any need to. As soon as I uttered my symbolic platitude, everyone nodded and smiled at me. They knew exactly what I meant.

Most of the time, though, the universal codes take on more complicated forms. When I called my brother after our father's death, my stepmother answered, and we had a conversation in which everything we said was an abstract gesture of aggression even though we uttered not one word of direct anger. Michiko started the exchange by saying, apropos of nothing, "So I suppose you will be staying at Akiko's house."

I knew right away that her comment was not a simple observation but a serious accusation. Even though Michiko did not want me to stay with her, I had insulted her by making my arrangements with my aunt without asking her first. My omission implied that her house was not good enough for me.

Instead of giving her a symbolic apology, I replied with another insult. "Of course I will stay at Aunt Akiko's. Listen, I called because I wanted to speak to my brother. When will he be home?" My remarks suggested that I had no intention of talking to Michiko, much less staying at her house.

We hung up soon after, neither of us saying it would be nice to get together or making remarks about staying healthy in the meantime. Though we didn't slam down our receivers or call each other names, our omission of these usual greetings added yet another insult.

In our conversation, what we did not say was as important

as what we said. The whole thing started because my choosing to stay at my aunt's house was a symbol of my allegiance: Akiko was my family, Michiko was not.

To neutralize this potent symbol, I was supposed to make
a show of indecisiveness. I was supposed to say to Michiko,
"I would love to stay at your house, but I hear it's a relatively
small apartment and Jumpei is already staying there. I don't
want to inconvenience you, so I'll ask Aunt Akiko. Do you
think she would mind?" Then Michiko could have said,
"You know you are always welcome here, but you are right,
maybe it would work out better if you went to Akiko's. Why
don't you call and ask her? I can't speak for her, to be sure,
but I don't think she would mind."

I had skipped over this whole process of pretending. It
would have been nice to say that I had done so because that
kind of empty ceremony is illogical and absurd, even hypo-
critical. But in talking to other relatives—especially my
grandmother, Fuku, whom I loved—I used to say plenty of
things that were illogical, absurd, and untrue, just to make
them feel better. I chose not to engage in double-talk with
Michiko because I didn't want to make her feel better at all.
If anything, I was pleased to make her feel slighted, so I used
the omission as a symbolic gesture—no different from stick-
ing out my tongue or pointing up my middle finger. Every
move I made was calculated to offend her. It was one of the
few times that I clearly understood what I was saying or not
saying in Japanese.

Symbols in Japan remind me of story problems in math and
dates in history. They are the things I should have learned
but didn't; they seem disconcertingly familiar and puzzling

at the same time. For me, the ultimate Japanese gesture/
symbol—one I have seen all my life and still don't really
"get"—is that of bowing.

As children in Japan, my brother and I seldom had to
bow. For children, the gesture was reserved for formal occasions like school ceremonies. We saw adults bowing to each
other almost every day, on the street or at the store, and we
laughed because the gesture looked funny and awkward.
Quite often, people straightened up from the bowing position too soon, discovered that the other person was still bent
down, and had to bow again. That floored us. It was better
than a comedy routine.

We were also amused to see adults—especially our
mother—bowing on the phone.

"Oh, I am so sorry," she would say, holding the receiver
tightly to her ear and lowering her head. "I didn't mean to
trouble you so much. I don't know how to thank you."

"Look," my brother and I would whisper to each other.
"She's bowing on the phone again. Doesn't she realize that
the other person can't see?"

The last time I saw my brother, we were at Michiko's
house, and someone called him on the phone. Since the
phone was only a few steps from where the rest of us were
having tea, I could hear his part of the conversation. It
sounded like a business call, probably from one of the customers for his wholesale store.

The caller did most of the talking, and my brother was
simply agreeing. "*Hai, hai,*" he said, over and over: "Yes,
yes." Every ten or twenty seconds, he said, "*Sumimasen,*"
which could mean "I'm sorry," "Thank you very much for
your trouble," "I'm glad you are doing me a favor," or all of

the above. Every time he said *Sumimasen* or another standard phrase, *Arigato gozaimasu*—"Thank you"—he pressed the receiver to his ear and bowed. He was doing the same thing our mother used to do, and speaking in a high, smooth voice, using all the levels of honorifics I had forgotten or never learned.

"One of the stores downtown," he told us after he hung up. He rolled his eyes. "I hate these people. They always drive such a hard bargain. They're dumb but aggressive. That guy who called is the worst of them all."

Jumpei had been forced to be polite to hold on to the caller's business—not because he liked or respected him. He wasn't embarrassed to criticize the caller behind his back, to admit that his own effusive gratitude and apologies had been insincere. If he was only pretending to be polite, I wondered, why did he make a physical gesture that the caller couldn't see? He could have been rolling his eyes and grimacing the whole time he was delivering polite apologies, as I probably would have—but instead, he had not only sounded but looked deeply grateful. I wasn't sure if the visual effect was strategic (his voice would not have sounded right without the physical gesture) or reflexive (he didn't even know that he was bowing).

I know that physical gestures are arbitrary codes and symbols in any culture. Handshakes and hugs are not the only expressions of good will. Still, some gestures and "body language" signals seem natural, instinctive, and universal. Even a dog will shake hands; my cats tap my face with their paws or jump up on my shoulder and rub their heads against my face when they want my attention. There is some universal urge—human and animal—to reach out and touch hands (or paws) and faces as expressions of affection and good will. Bowing seems a little more abstract, a little further removed from the physical or instinctual. You can train a dog to shake hands, to sit, to retrieve balls, even to sing on command; gorillas have been taught to use computer keyboards or to sign for words. Though perhaps it is possible, I cannot imagine Koko and Michael bowing to each other.

Bowing confuses me because it looks like a gesture of submission—like a dog rolling over or hanging its head in front of the owner—and yet it isn't. When two women meet on the street and bow to each other, it's hard to say who's submitting to whom: submission is usually one-sided, not mutual. Besides, gestures of submission and dominance come with a visceral feeling. They are not detached and ambiguous in the way bowing is.

A few years ago, Chuck went to visit an old high school friend, Mike, and the two of them ended up having a drink at a "motorcycle bar." It was a bar where Mike had previously gotten into a few fights, all of which he had won. While Chuck and Mike were drinking beer at the counter, two young men in black leather jackets came up to them.

"It was clear they wanted to pick a fight," Chuck told me later. "They stood next to Mike, squared their shoulders, and grunted. Mike immediately stood up and asked them what they wanted. He was standing tall, looking like a muscleman. A few more words were exchanged, which I couldn't hear. The music was pretty loud. But I could feel myself sitting up straighter and looking right at these guys. The four of us stared at one another, two against two. Nobody moved. After a few seconds, Mike sat down, the guys went away, and then all night those two guys kept coming back and wanting to shake our hands. Every half hour, they would come up to us and shake our hands. It was weird. All this time, because I hadn't realized we were going to a motorcycle bar, I had on my Reebok aerobic shoes. Everyone else was wearing cowboy boots of course. I couldn't stand up because I didn't want these guys to see my shoes. When we left, Mike said, 'Here we were about to get into a fight and you had on your ballerina shoes.' "

Even though Chuck has never gotten into a barroom fight, he wasn't at all confused by what happened at the bar. The two guys wanted to challenge Mike because he was like the lead dog or the top gorilla. Mike asserted his dominance by standing up right away, squaring his shoulders, and asking the men what they wanted. He was accepting their challenge and calling their bluff. Discouraged from repeating the challenge, the two guys had to make periodic gestures of peace, the way dogs roll over in front of their pack leader. But the whole thing would have been different if the two guys had seen what "sissy" shoes Chuck had on—they would not have conceded Mike's dominance if his "buddy" was wearing "ballerina shoes."

The event Chuck told me about is completely bizarre and completely understandable; the behavior of the men in the bar is like something out of a bad TV show: theatrical, stereotypical, and so easy to interpret. When I think of my brother bowing on the phone, I feel the exact reverse. As he stood by the couch bowing and apologizing to a person he couldn't see, he was like a character from the folk tales whose "moral" always eluded me when our mother read them to us—the Peach Boy, the Fisherman Who Rescued the Sea Tortoise, the Raccoon Who Fooled a Buddhist Priest by Pretending to Be a Kettle. I had known him all my life, and yet he was an enigma: he was like a literary symbol I could not understand.

SCHOOL

⁜

During our senior year at college, some of my classmates said they could hardly wait to graduate, to join "the real world." They couldn't concentrate on classes, knowing that they would soon be out of school forever. I didn't feel the same way at all. School seemed as "real" to me as "the outside world"—only more interesting.

I still don't trust the distinction often made between school and "the real world," which implies that there is something insubstantial or artificial about school. The business meetings I attended in Milwaukee as an interpreter confirmed my suspicion that arcane and "academic" discussions don't happen only at colleges. The directors of two small companies, one Japanese and the other American, once had a twenty-minute debate about whether the plastic cover of a particular camera lens should be "pumpkin yellow" or "the yellow of raincoats." What each man meant by these terms was unclear to the other and had to be redefined many times over. This is the conversation I recall now when I attend academic conferences and cannot understand what is being said about a book I have read more than once.

School and "the real world" both have their absurd moments, but school is where people go when they are not satisfied with their "real world" lives and want a change. Many Americans in their thirties and forties go back to college to get trained for a different line of work or to pursue a lifelong interest they couldn't afford to study earlier. Until they are in need of such second chances, most Americans take colleges for granted because they are always there—almost any adult can get into some college at any age.

Being able to go back to school is a particularly American opportunity. My Japanese friends will never be able to do the same. In Japan, school does not give anyone a second chance. Many of my Japanese friends are married women with money who already have college degrees. But none of them can go back to college to earn a second degree in art, education, or social work, as their American counterparts may do.

Recently, a few Japanese colleges have started accepting applications from adults who have been out of school for years, but these colleges are exceptions. The only way most people can get into a college in Japan is to take and pass the entrance examination for that particular college immediately after graduating from high school. The number of exams a student can sit for in a given year is limited since many schools give their exams on the same day.

A student who does not get into any college will have to wait a year, attending a cram school. There is a word for a student in this situation—ronin (floating person). In feudal times, the word referred to samurai whose clan had been dissolved. Feudal ronin had to roam around until they could find a new master to serve. To be a modern ronin is scarcely better: while their friends move on to colleges or jobs, ronin must float around for a year without any allegiance. In Japan, anyone who doesn't belong to the right group at the right time feels like a failure. If a ronin can't get into a college after a year at a cram school, he or she usually gives up and settles for a low-paying job rather than spending another year floating around.

In the States, young people who don't feel ready for college can work for a few years and then apply when they feel more motivated or mature. Young Japanese people don't have the same chance. For older adults to go back to school to have a second chance—at a job or an artistic career or personal fulfillment—is practically impossible.

The very accessibility of schools in America adds to the perception that they are not real or substantial enough. Many Americans who criticize their own school system for being "too easy" idealize the Japanese school system because they are drawn to its tough image. The details Americans cite as the merits of the Japanese system actually reflect their ideal of the mythical "real world" where people must work hard—long hours, the emphasis on discipline and basic skills, the tough competition among peers. These people admire the Japanese school system because they see it as a samurai version of their own fantasies about the American work ethic.

My education at a traditional Japanese grade school was

nothing so glorious. Day-to-day life at a Japanese public school was harsh but also boring. Until I transferred to a private school in seventh grade, I didn't learn anything that I couldn't have learned at home by reading and memorizing the same books with my mother's help.

Recently when I was in Japan, I was asked why I did not write my novels in Japanese, why I did not at least translate my own work. The question surprised me at first. The people who asked knew that for twelve years I have lived in a small Wisconsin town where I have few opportunities to speak Japanese. No one can write novels in a language she has not spoken every day for more than a decade. But there is another reason I could not possibly have written my novels or poems in Japanese: I was never taught to write in what was my native language. My public education in Japan prepared me to make the correct letters to spell out the correct sounds, but that is not the same as teaching me how to write.

When I started the first grade at six, I had not been taught to read at home—at least not in a formal way. Because my mother read to me all the time, I had memorized my favorite books and could read along with her. Sometimes, when my mother and I were standing on the street corner waiting for a taxi, I noticed that I could read the license plates of the cars passing by. I would read the plates and she would nod and smile because I was right, but no big fuss was made about my being able to read. Most of the other kids starting school with me were the same way: we sort of knew how to read because of our mothers, but we hadn't been formally trained.

In first grade, we were taught the fifty phonetic signs that make up the Japanese alphabet, a dozen simple pictorial characters, and the basic numbers. By the end of the year, everyone in our class could read our textbooks and write simple messages to our family and friends in our sprawling, uneven handwriting. People who admire the Japanese education system are partially right. Japanese schools *are* very good at teaching skills like basic writing—which can only be learned through memorization and repeated practice.

Once we learned the alphabet and some pictorial characters, my classmates and I wrote compositions about our families, our vacations, our friends. Occasionally, our teachers had us write stories and poems as well. In summer, we were given notebooks in which we had to keep "picture diaries": on the upper, blank, half we drew pictures, and on the lower, lined, half we wrote sentences about what we did every day. These assignments gave us a lot of practice at writing.

When we got to the upper grades, though, our assignments changed. We no longer wrote stories or poems; our compositions weren't about our personal experiences or feelings. Almost every writing assignment was a book report or a summary of our reading. We had to follow a very strict formula, organizing our thoughts under predetermined headings like "plot," "characters," "setting," "themes," "what we learned from the book." If we didn't follow the format, we got poor grades.

The grades didn't always make sense. Luckily, I did well most of the time, but I wasn't sure what I did right aside from adhering to the format. The only suggestions I got were circled corrections where I had used the wrong pictorial characters or general remarks about my bad penmanship.

A few of my friends didn't do so well, but they were never given suggestions for improvement. They would simply get low grades and comments like "Your writing needs improvement," "You didn't really follow the directions for the assignment," or "I can see you tried some but you still have a long way to go." Often, our teachers openly scolded pupils. In front of the whole class, my friends were told to "pay better attention" and to "try harder." It didn't matter that most of them were serious and well-behaved students, not lazy and inattentive troublemakers; they were already trying hard, trying to pay attention.

No matter what the subject, our teachers never gave us very clear advice about how to do better. When I couldn't understand long division or fractions and decimals in math, I felt bad at first. On the timed tests we had every day, I could finish only half the problems before the teacher's stopwatch beeped, telling us to put down our pencils. The results were put up on the wall, and my name was always near the bottom. I was told to "try harder," but none of my teachers spent extra time with me to go over what I was doing wrong. Since I wasn't given a real chance to improve, I decided after a while that I didn't really care how I did.

Over and over again, our Japanese education offered this sort of harsh judgment combined with vague exhortation. In every subject, kids who didn't do well were made to feel ashamed and yet given no chance to improve. The humiliation was especially obvious in physical education classes. At our grade school we were expected to learn to swim in the same way we were expected to learn to write:

by sheer repetition and "trying harder." We were left to swim around on our own, but the pool hours weren't just for fun. Each of us had to wear a cloth swim-cap with the symbol that indicated our skill level. Students who couldn't swim at all were singled out by the big red circle sewn on top of their caps. "Red mark, red mark, you'll sink like a big hammer," some of the other kids taunted, and the teachers did nothing to stop them. I was glad that I already knew how to swim by the time I started school.

For those of us who could swim, there were monthly tests to determine how far we could go without stopping. For every five or ten meters we could swim, our mothers sewed red or black lines on the side of our caps. Those who could swim fifty meters in the crawl, sidestroke, or breaststroke got the best marks on their caps: five all-black lines. In fifth grade, when I passed the test for fifty meters, my teachers praised me for having "tried so hard," even though I was able to do so well only because my mother had taught me to swim in the river near her parents' home. Unlike my teachers, my mother enjoyed giving specific instructions. She drew diagrams on paper to show me what my arms and legs should be doing for crawl and sidestroke. Then she made me lie down on the sand on the river bank to practice the arm and leg movements. Once I was in the water, she stood on the bank shouting out instructions like "Stretch your arms all the way," "Turn your head sideways." When my form was wrong, she showed me by imitating me—exaggerating my awkward movements and making me laugh. "I don't look like that," I protested, but I knew exactly what I needed to improve.

I did not learn how to write in Japanese because even at the private school I attended after seventh grade, Japanese language classes were taught by older men who had studied classical Japanese literature or Chinese poetry at the national universities before the war. They were the most conservative and traditional of all our teachers. In their classes, we read the works of famous authors and wrote essays to answer questions like: "What is the theme?" "When does the main character realize the importance of morality?" "What important Buddhist philosophy is expressed in this passage?" All the writing we did for our extracurricular activities—for skits or school newspapers and magazines—was supervised by younger teachers who did not teach Japanese.

During those same years, we learned how to write in English. Our English teachers were young Japanese women who had studied in the States or England, and American women from small Midwestern towns who had just graduated from college. In their classes, we wrote essays about our families, friends, hobbies, future dreams—personal subjects we had not written about at school since third grade. We were given plenty of instruction about the specifics of writing: word choice, description, style. Our essays came back with comments both about our writing and about the thoughts we had expressed. I looked forward to writing essays and reading my teachers' comments. By the time I was a high school senior, I wanted to be a writer, and English was the only language I could write in.

To study writing, I had to go to an American college. Creative writing was not—and still is not—offered at Japanese colleges, in English or in Japanese. I don't know how

Japanese writers learn to write, since most of them, as children, must have had the same kind of education I had. There are no schools or writers' conferences where a person can study creative writing as an adult. I have never heard of people getting together to form a writing group or workshop.

Writing is not something that comes naturally to the chosen few. Most American writers of my generation didn't just learn to write on their own. Without the classes we took in creative writing and modern literature, we wouldn't have known what to read, how to read it, how to pay attention to form and content. We needed to be shown how to write good dialogue, smooth transitions, pared-down but vivid character descriptions. These things didn't come naturally. It would have taken us thirty years to learn, on our own, the same skills we learned in eight years of college and graduate school. My friends at graduate school came from average Midwestern homes; they were not children of famous writers. School gave us a chance we would never have had otherwise. In America, we are proof that the romantic notion of the natural writer is a myth. In Japan, where no formal training is offered in writing, the myth may be a sad reality that prevents many people from becoming writers.

My stepmother used the traditional method of harsh judgment even though she was not a teacher. When Michiko came to live with my family, I was twelve and already knew how to cook and bake simple foods like omelettes and chocolate chip cookies and how to clean up the kitchen. But my attempts to help Michiko always ended in disaster. She complained endlessly about how I had not been taught to do things the "proper way." Everything I did, from drying the dishes to sweeping the floor, was wrong. "I can't believe that you don't know how to do this," she would scold in her shrill voice, and yet she never showed me exactly what the "proper way" was. When I asked, "What do you mean? What am I doing wrong?" she would scream, "If I have to tell you, then it's no good. I can't show you something you should already know." I was supposed to watch her silently and learn on my own through observation, but she made me too nervous to concentrate. I had no idea what I was supposed to be looking for. If I gave up and asked, "Do you mean the way I am holding the broom or are you saying that I should start over there instead of here?" she would stomp out of the kitchen without a word.

I know that Michiko's silent and judgmental manner was a manifestation of her meanspiritedness, but she didn't invent the method. The tradition of not giving specific instruction comes from Zen. In traditional Zen philosophy, satori or enlightenment is considered to be beyond human description. Since no one can describe satori or ways to attain it, the teacher-monk asks his disciples a series of koans—questions meant to puzzle and disturb rather than to provide answers. The whole purpose of the koan is to break down the disciples' reliance on their own intellect by humiliating them. At its worst, the teaching technique amounts to intellectual or spiritual hazing. The disciples are supposed to hit bottom and suffer terrible despair before they can open their eyes to satori and experience beauty and peace that is beyond logic or description.

To my American friends who took up Zen in college, this style of teaching seemed liberating because of its apparent emphasis on a larger and unexplainable truth instead of minute and trivial details. After years of American education, my friends were tired of specific instruction. All the rules they had to learn about writing good paragraphs or improving their tennis swings struck them as fussy and superficial. Zen taught them that everything they had learned in their Western education was an illusion that needed to be shattered. The very destructiveness and uncertainty of enlightenment sounded uplifting.

But in the Zen-style teaching actually practiced in Japan, students are not liberated from minute details. The details are everything. A beginning calligraphy student writes the same letters over and over, trying to make her brush strokes look exactly like her master's. If she puts one dot five millimeters too far to the right, her work is considered flawed. The master does not point out her mistake. "No, not right yet," he grunts. "Do it over." Until the student can see for herself that her dot is in the wrong place, she will have to keep copying the same letters—she has not reached "enlightenment."

In America, students are often drilled on the details of grammar or form and yet are forgiven for the minor mistakes they make in their writing. Their teacher might say, "You have a couple of awkward sentences and punctuation mistakes here, but your paper is excellent overall. Your ideas are good and you write with a wonderful voice." Hearing comments like these, my friends concluded that their teachers were being inconsistent. If the minor details weren't important in the end, why did the teachers spend so much time on them?

The paradox about the two styles of teaching is that neither emphasizes what it considers to be truly important. In calligraphy and other traditional arts derived from Zen, following the correct form is everything—there is no possibility that you can make a few minor mistakes and still "get" the spirit or the essence of the "truth"—and yet instruction consists of vague exhortation about "following the right balance" and "working hard." In America, where teachers actually value the overall spirit of the work, they spend most of their time talking about details.

This paradox reflects a common ground all teachers share. No matter what and how we teach, we believe that what we value the most is beyond our meager ability to describe. We are struck dumb with admiration at the things we value, so we try to teach the secondary things that we think are easier to talk about. Like most American writing teachers, I value the overall spirit or genuine voice in my students' work and yet nag them about the smaller details of technique like trimming their lines or writing better dialogue. Mine is a Western approach—the same method of instruction is apparent even in the Bible, which gives God a name that cannot be spoken, while offering book after book detailing the laws about how to build a temple or what foods should not be eaten together.

My Japanese teachers, who thought that detail was everything, must have felt that precision was so important that it could not be described: only the truly enlightened can be in perfect harmony with the correct form. In the meantime, they must have reasoned, they could at least talk about the value of hard work, something everyone can easily understand. The contradiction we share points to the difficulty of teaching anything: trying to pass on knowledge that seems so clear to ourselves to people who don't have that knowledge. When my stepmother complained, "How can I teach you something you should already know?" she was expressing in its meanest form the universal frustration of teachers.

In spite of our shared frustration, though, I have a hard time forgiving some of my former teachers in Japan because they never seemed humbled by the near impossibility of their task. Many of my teachers felt entitled to be both strict and arbitrary—strict about their own authority and the rules of the system and yet so arbitrary and lax about helping us.

In Japan, whether you are in school or at your private karate, judo, or *ikebana* lesson, you can never question the authority of the teacher, whom you address simply as "sensei," literally, "one whose life comes first." Unless there are multiple teachers who need to be distinguished from one another, you do not even use their family names, much less first names (which you most likely do not know). The teacher is like the biblical God, whom you cannot name.

Students are not expected to question the competence of their teachers or the usefulness of their assignments, any more than Zen disciples can rebel against their master and his koans. Japanese students who study at American universities are amazed that at the end of the semester most universities ask their students to evaluate their teachers. Even though students in Japan complain to each other about their teachers, they would never think of writing an evaluation or filing official grievances.

In the teaching of many traditional Japanese art forms, the teacher's authority is backed up by a complex hierarchy called *ie* that controls instruction. Even the choice of this word, since it means both "house" and "family origin," reflects high expectations of allegiance. What is described in English as a "school" (such as a school of writing or painting) is actually a "family" in Japanese. Each *ie* is structured like a family hierarchy: at the top is the head teacher, called *iemoto* (source of the house), and under him are various assistant teachers who, in turn, take their own assistants. All these teachers are licensed by the *ie*. A beginner in *ikebana* or Japanese dance will study with a minor assistant teacher for a few years and then move on to a more advanced teacher. There are various levels of competence awarded along the way, but every advancement must be approved by the *ie*.

The system makes it impossible for a student to challenge any teacher's decision, since the teacher can invoke the authority of the whole clanlike hierarchy. Teachers can make any arbitrary decision so long as it can be backed up by the *ie*. When my cousin Kazumi studied *ikebana*, she was disillusioned by the unfair judgments her teachers made every year about who should be allowed to advance to the next level of competence. There were no tests or lists of tasks and qualities that determined the advancements. Who advanced and who didn't seemed entirely up to the teachers' whims. People who were related to any of the teachers rose through the ranks much faster than those who weren't.

Whether or not they won an advancement to the next level, all the students were required to attend the annual certificate ceremony in their best kimonos. The year of the Kobe earthquake Kazumi received a letter from her *ie* advising students to rent a good kimono to attend the annual ceremony if theirs had been destroyed in the earthquake.

"I had been disillusioned with *ikebana* for some time anyway," Kazumi told me, "but the letter was the last straw. I couldn't believe that the teachers thought this was a time for people to be worrying about their kimonos. Even though the letter said that we didn't necessarily have to have a nice kimono if our family had suffered such a great damage that we had no money, the tone was very condescending—and it was obvious that they were really saying that we should rent one no matter what the cost. They didn't write and say, 'We are so sorry about the earthquake. We would be so happy if you could still come to the annual ceremony in spite of the damage many of you must have suffered, and of course, you can wear whatever you would like.' "

She switched to Dutch-style flower arrangement even though it, too, has a nationwide association that oversees its teaching and licensing. Like *ikebana*, Dutch flower arrangement has different levels of teachers and different levels of competence, but Kazumi sees a big difference between the two. To advance from one to the next in the Dutch style, people take tests in which each person is given a bucket of flowers to make into a table arrangement, a small bouquet, and a corsage; a group of judges scores the results. Everybody has the same amount of time, the same number of arrangements to complete, similar flowers in the bucket, and the same group of judges. Evaluation isn't arbitrary the way it was for *ikebana*. In the lessons she took—mostly from Dutch teachers—plenty of specific instruction was given about colors, textures, shapes, and the flowers themselves. Her teachers looked at her work and gave her suggestions— something none of her *ikebana* teachers ever did.

Until I talked to Kazumi, I was hoping that even though my Japanese friends could not go back to school in their thirties and forties, they might be able to take private lessons or receive training through volunteer work in order to pursue some of their interests. Even in small towns like Green Bay, many people my age can learn new skills, pursue their hobbies, or work for causes they believe in without enrolling in school.

My Japanese friends do not have similar chances to learn something new or feel useful. There are very few volunteer organizations in Japan for nature conservation, crisis intervention, helping children, or working with families who are poor or homeless. The few soup kitchens one might find in big Japanese cities are operated by international organizations like the Salvation Army. People who work at them are mostly foreigners. A nice Japanese housewife is not expected to do volunteer work for strangers. "If she has time to help people she doesn't even know," her relatives would grumble, "why doesn't she do more to help her own kids study? Why doesn't she run for an office in the P.T.A. at their school?" Most middle-class Japanese people seem to think that poor people deserve to be poor—it's their own fault or the fault of their families and relatives. Nobody should expect help from total strangers. As for conserving nature, that is the job of biologists. My friends have a hard time justifying their passion for gardening to their husbands and in-laws. If they were to spend their afternoons taking care of injured wildlife or clearing marshes of trash instead of cleaning their houses and preparing special meals for their children, their families would probably disown them.

Nice housewives like my friends can take private lessons only if they can be justified as genteel means of cultivating fine, feminine tastes—like *ikebana*, tea, koto and samisen music—but these are the traditional Japanese arts with the strict *ie* structure. Joining the *ie* would involve my friends in another burdensome system of duties and obligations, something they already experience in every facet of their lives.

In so many ways, Japan is a place of no second chances. Many of my friends are in very unhappy marriages. They write to me about the shouting and shoving matches they have with their husbands, about the night they tried to run away, only to have the husband chase them down the street, catch them, and drag them home. Unable to run away, my friends lock themselves up in the guest room or sleep in their daughters' rooms to avoid sleeping with their husbands. For most American women, leaving a bad marriage like theirs would be nothing but happiness. My friends stay because divorce still carries a big stigma in Japan. If they leave their husbands, they may never be able to see their children again. Certainly, they will not be able to marry again and try another chance at marriage. Nobody marries a divorced middle-aged woman in Japan.

Life in Japan is like an unending stint at a school where you have to keep taking tests—giving your answers under pressure without help or guidance, knowing that you will get no second chance if you make a mistake. Japanese people have to make many of the big decisions of their lives—whom to marry, what company to join—without detailed information, since it is rude to ask direct questions even at *omiai* meetings and job interviews. They have no choice but to trust authority and do their best, just as they were supposed to do in school. If their job or marriage turns out to be a disappointment, they will be given the same vague exhortations they heard from their teachers: keep trying, work hard, pay attention.

There is nothing intrinsically wrong with trying harder. Sometimes when I see my former students in Green Bay seeming to flounder—waiting on tables or working clerical jobs they hate, the whole time talking about their big plans to "go back to school" soon—I think maybe a little Japanese perseverance might not hurt them. I know that for them or for anyone else, going back to school does not guarantee a job or happiness. Within school, too, when my students complain that everything we read in a modern American literature class is depressing or that I simply do not "like" their work (when every poem they wrote in the class is a love poem in couplets), I long for a little Japanese respect for authority. Some of my students would be better off if they trusted me a little rather than questioning my decisions at every turn. Still, I would rather have students who question too much than those who assume that I know best and don't owe them any explanations. No one should have power that is unjustified and unjustifiable, regardless of how convenient or efficient it may seem for the smooth running of the classroom, the educational system, or the country.

The problem with the Japanese system, ultimately, is that individual freedom—to question the teacher, to disagree—is sacrificed for the supposed convenience and protection of the whole group. The system works well for people who feel no desire to rebel. The Japanese ie system my cousin complained about does ensure that anyone who perseveres in a given art form will have some recognition; periodically, every student is asked to take part in public exhibitions or concerts. Most Japanese students have public-performance opportunities many of my American friends—artists and musicians—don't.

But for me—as well as for my cousin—the price is too high. The security comes with too many obligations. The *ie* system asks that you trust your teachers who have not earned or deserved your trust. What you are required to have is blind faith in the *ie*: like the church or the mosque, the *ie* is an institution that is designed to inspire total obedience to its rules. In Japan, if you reject your chance to enjoy the security that comes from joining the right group such as an *ie*, an elite school, a good company, or a respectable family, you will have to leave the country or live in it as an outcast. Life in Japan resembles the harshest interpretation of a religious faith: the Koran or the sword, either you are with Christ or against him, either you join the sheltering umbrella of Japanese security or you have nothing. In school and elsewhere, people are rewarded for obeying the rules diligently, never for taking a chance and being different, or for asking good questions.

But words like *security* and *uncertainty* are misleading. Because Dutch-style flower arrangement is not as popular as *ikebana* and the association does not provide the same kind of protection that a traditional *ie* gives its teachers, my cousin is struggling to get enough students for the classes she offers. She has quit her clerical job, which she did not like, and committed herself to the life of a flower-arrangement teacher. She isn't going to get a second chance at being a clerk or going back to *ikebana*. My cousin's life is uncertain and insecure. But daily, as she arranges her own flowers and watches her students cutting and arranging theirs, she is certain of other things. She knows when she is making a good arrangement and when she is not. In Dutch-style arrangements, my cousin has learned what colors and shapes look pleasing; she has a firm sense of what she considers beautiful. She also knows that she will tell her students exactly what she thinks about their work rather than keeping her criticism to herself or being vague. Kazumi feels a certainty about truth, beauty, honesty. That is the only certainty worth choosing.

TEARS

❊

A few days after our father's death, Jumpei told me that he had cried at the funeral.

"It was a big funeral. Six hundred people came," my brother said. "The man who gave the eulogy broke down and cried at the podium. He had been Father's right-hand man at the office. The man said that Father was the most generous person he had ever met. There were hundreds of young women who must have been secretaries and data processors. All of them were crying. I got choked up just watching them cry. It was *morai-naki* for me." He tipped his head back and laughed.

Morai-naki (to receive crying) refers to the way a person is moved to tears by watching others cry even though he or she has no personal reason to feel sad. It seemed peculiar that my brother, the only son, should think of his own tears at the funeral as a stranger's tears. But I understood. My brother and I weren't as close to our father as were the women who held temporary clerical jobs at his office. We didn't know the "generous" man his co-workers mourned. To us, Hiroshi was a scary character from our childhood. We had spent our adulthood trying to avoid him—living as far away from him as possible. Even while he was alive, Hiroshi seemed more like a bad memory than a real person.

"Father was such a strange character," Jumpei said.

I nodded. We were in a cab. I had just arrived from Green Bay and my brother had met me at the airport. Now we were headed for our aunt's house, where I was to stay for a week. In the rearview mirror, I glimpsed the eyes of the driver and wondered if he had been listening to our conversation. The driver appeared to be fifty-five, sixty—almost our father's age. He could have been appalled by how unfilial my brother and I sounded, but his eyes showed no emotion.

My brother continued talking as if the two of us were alone. No one in Japan expects a cab driver to show—or even experience—any emotions in the presence of his customers. That is part of the paradox about emotions in Japan. We are taught to refrain from expressing our feelings in public because to do so is rude, intrusive, and selfish; and yet it is all right for six hundred people to cry together at a funeral, or for an important company official to break down in public in the middle of delivering a eulogy. To start crying at the sight of other people's tears may be a common human response, but not every culture has a name for it. In Japan, morai-naki is an accepted form of crying that merits its own name.

Morai-naki is acceptable because community is everything. If everyone is crying at a gathering, you should, too. Certain public rituals—funerals, grave visits, other Buddhist ceremo-

nies related to death—are set aside as occasions for everyone's tears, for mass displays of emotions, while private,
individual tears (and displays of other emotions) are considered inappropriate and embarrassing. In Japan, you can cry
all you want in a group. Crying is often the most appropriate
public gesture you can make.

The distinction between public gestures and private feelings
affects the Japanese attitude toward death, especially chosen
death. Japanese history offers many examples of honorable
suicide. As a child, I watched numerous historical dramas on
TV in which a brave samurai would commit seppuku to
avoid being captured by the enemy, or as a form of apology
for letting down his master. Honorable suicide was not reserved for men. Princesses and other noble women cut their
throats or swallowed poison to avoid being captured by or
married off to the enemy. This kind of suicide was carried
out as a public ritual—men and women dressed in their best
white robes to express their purity and killed themselves in
the presence of witnesses.

Although the TV movies were dramatizations, many of
them were based on historical events from feudal times.
There have even been a few instances of ritual suicide in
modern times, the best-known being the writer Yukio
Mishima. Mishima and his followers stormed into one of the
headquarters of the Japanese Self-Defense Army and held a
general hostage. After delivering a long speech about honor,
duty, and the samurai tradition, Mishima committed seppuku in the presence of his followers. Even though some
people considered Mishima to be a fanatic, no one thought
that his suicide was a shameful and embarrassing event to be

covered up. At worst, his death was seen as a misguided public gesture, a crazy attempt to deliver his message about honor and glory.

When my mother decided to end her life, she was making the same choice as the samurai or the noble women: not to continue a life she considered unworthy and unhappy. But nobody saw it that way. Even my mother's family did not console me by saying, "Your mother believed that she was making the only dignified choice possible. You don't have to agree with her, but you must try to understand and forgive." No one encouraged me to talk or think about what my mother might have been thinking or feeling. My uncles and maternal grandfather burned incense in silence. My aunts and grandmother said very vaguely, "Your mother was very unhappy. You have to be strong and try to live a happy life so she can rest in peace." From the way they looked at me, their lips pursed, their eyes downcast, I knew they did not want to continue what could only be a painful discussion. My father and paternal grandfather were less kind. They told me that my mother's suicide had shamed our family, that I was never to mention the event because if people found out about this disgrace, my brother and I would never be able to marry or get a job. Though my aunts and grandmother meant well and my father and paternal grandfather did not, they agreed on one thing: my mother's suicide was too horrible to be discussed. Her action was an expression of private despair, not a public gesture, so it was shameful instead of glorious.

The distinction between the private and the public also influences the Japanese attitude toward tragedy as an art form. Almost all the famous Japanese plays from the nineteenth century and before are tragedies about lovers who kill themselves together because they cannot marry (there is a Japanese word for this type of double suicide: *shinju*—literally, "inside the heart") or faithful servants who sacrifice their lives to avenge their master's death (*Chushingura* is the most famous version of this story). These plays are a public ritual: coming together to see them, people can cry and express their emotions without shame or embarrassment.

In Japan, where close friends or family struggle never to cry in front of one another, there is no embarrassment about crying at theaters or in front of the TV set. My father claimed not to have shed a tear at his own mother's deathbed, but he often sat with wet eyes in front of the TV, late at night, watching some cheap love story. Audiences at traditional Kabuki or *joruri* (puppet theater) cry without inhibition. The less emotional, more abstract Noh theater does not have the same popular following as Kabuki and *joruri*. American movies that become box-office hits in Japan are Hollywood tearjerkers like *Love Story, Gone With the Wind, A Star Is Born*. The same people who cry at these movies would be totally embarrassed if they saw your eyes fill with tears while you were having coffee with them.

Many of my Midwestern friends—especially men—are the same way. They refrain from crying in front of their close friends when they are sad about something private, and yet, in the middle of a mediocre movie, they are not embarrassed to sniffle. The only difference is that while Midwesterners may be unwilling to cry, they won't politely look away when someone does.

If I cried in front of my Midwestern friends, they would

hand me a tissue, ask me if I was all right, and try to make me laugh. Humor is a common Midwestern antidote to sadness. I often find myself resorting to it. At the funeral of our colleague's mother, one of my friends started crying as soon as we entered the church and saw the coffin by the altar. My friend had recently lost both his parents, but he felt silly about crying since he hadn't known the woman who had died (too bad he wasn't in Japan—he could have explained his crying as *morai-naki*, which it was). My friend tried to make light of his tears, calling himself a "big wimp." As I sat down next to him, I didn't lean over and hug him or encourage him to talk. I made some wisecrack about how churches should be equipped with boxes of Kleenex tucked between the hymnals and missals. I was only doing what I was supposed to do as a friend—help him downplay his sadness by turning it into a good-natured joke. A note of cheerfulness is valued in the Midwest, just as quiet dignity is valued in Japan.

My own feelings about crying are a confused mixture of values and behaviors I have learned and those I rebelled against. I don't enjoy crying, alone or in front of people, but if I had to, I would rather cry with a few close friends than in a large crowd of strangers or all alone. I feel too self-conscious to bawl in a public place, and yet I am not one to indulge in a good solitary cry. In the last years of her life, my mother cried all day by herself—I know this from her diary as well as from my memories of her red eyes—so I think of solitary crying as a sign of great unhappiness, a warning that I should seek help. Some of my friends think of crying alone as a catharsis, but I hate the choked-up feeling tears cause, the way crying hurts my throat and nose and blocks my breathing. Even alone, I feel a little foolish for carrying on.

The public catharsis of crying at a movie theater seems even more silly and unnecessary. A few years ago, a group of my friends went to see *The Joy Luck Club* without inviting me because they thought the movie would be too upsetting for me, since one of the main characters loses her mother to suicide. They didn't know that I had already seen it with Chuck.

When Chuck and I arrived at the theater, an earlier show was just ending, so we stood outside the doors, which were open. As the credits rolled on the screen, we could hear people sniffling and blowing their noses in the dark and trying to gather their purses and jackets and keys. We didn't dare look at each other, for fear of bursting into embarrassed giggles. There was a smaller audience for the later show, but twenty minutes into it, almost everyone was crying. Again, we heard people sniffling and blowing their nose and sucking in their breath. When our eyes met, we could no longer contain ourselves. We sat there laughing quietly, trying not to let on, because it seemed rude to laugh when other people were crying.

My friends said they had cried throughout the movie and were surprised to hear about my reaction. But I have never cried at a movie in my life. Just when I feel a little sad, everyone starts crying, and that makes me want to laugh. Crying with a group of people requires perfect timing. If you miss the right moment, you can only feel stupid, like someone who missed the punch line of a joke.

I did cry, though, when I read Amy Tan's book, upon

which the movie was based. It wasn't the weeping kind of a catharsis that people were having at the movie. Being moved by a book is a quiet experience. One of the books that made me cry was Kazuo Ishiguro's *The Remains of the Day*. The narrator, a British butler, and I had nothing in common, and I didn't find him entirely likable. All the same, I cried when he admitted that his heart was breaking as the woman he had come to see was boarding the bus to leave him. What made me cry was not the butler and his situation but the words and the sentences Ishiguro had written for him—how inevitably one word followed another as the narrator was forced to confront a painful revelation.

I was moved by the way Ishiguro had arranged those words and sentences so that the essential moment stood out and seemed so starkly *there*. My tears are for the author rather than for the characters, the situation, or the story. Reading a good book is like watching an Olympic athlete: I cry because the writer's performance is as beautiful and perfect as the athelete's. Perhaps for this reason, almost all the books that make me cry are written by my contemporaries. Much as I love Jane Austen, Shakespeare, or John Donne, I am not moved to tears across the long, blank stretch of time. What fills me with awe is the fact that someone who is living at the same time as I—someone who shares my world—can write so beautifully.

In Japan, the English adjectives *wet* and *soft* are often used to describe people who are sensitive and emotional, while *hard* and *dry* mean being practical and rational. People I meet on business there, especially the journalists who interview me about my books, are always astonished that I am so "hard and dry." Because I have written about loss, sadness, and family tragedy, I am assumed to be a very sensitive person or even a dark tormented soul. People are disappointed by how cheerful, ordinary, and ultimately boring I am. I am not the tragic character they hoped to encounter.

There is nothing inherently emotional about being a writer or an artist, but both in Japan and in America, many people like to envision artists as sensitive souls in the grip of wild sorrows and joys. A few years ago, when my friend Kate started painting, a mutual friend wrote to her and praised her in what we thought was an over-dramatic way. He commended her for trying to find joy in the true nature of things, for wanting to be one with beauty. He encouraged her to let her heart be filled with whatever she was feeling, to trust her emotions. Kate laughed and said, "You know, when I'm on that path by the river with my sketch pad, I'm not thinking these big thoughts. I don't say to myself, 'I must open my heart to the true nature of things.' No, I'm thinking, 'I hope I remembered to bring some bug spray.' I hate bugs."

A few days after she received this letter, Kate and I stopped at a rummage sale in a small town, where she found a fold-up stool. It was perfect for her outdoor sketching. She bought the stool and looked forward to using it on the next sunny day.

Kate and I are too practical to regard our "art" as an emotional catharsis. We are more concerned about bug sprays and fold-up stools that won't fall apart when we sit down.

I haven't always been the practical and even-tempered person I am now. On a recent trip to Japan, I was forced to remember the crybaby I used to be. Our old neighbor, Mrs. Kuzuha, reminded me while I was having dinner with her.

"You came running to me every time you and Tadashi had a fight. You'd say, 'Obachan, Tadashi said a mean thing to me,' 'Tadashi pushed me,' 'Tadashi won't let me read his book,' and you'd cry. I always took your side and told Tadashi to be more considerate." She laughed. "You were cute. I envied your mother for having a daughter as well as a son."

"You envied her for having a couple of crybabies as kids?"

"No. You were both such nice children."

Jumpei and I might have been nice children in our own ways, but we were the biggest crybabies in our neighborhood. When we bickered, he would cry and say that I had been mean to him. Then I would have to be "nice" to him because I was the older one. Even though I resented my brother for getting his way by crying, that didn't stop me from doing the same thing to Mrs. Kuzuha's sons—Makoto, who was three years older, and Tadashi, who was my age but taller and bigger. I cried and tattled on them and fully expected Mrs. Kuzuha to take my side.

A few days after I saw Mrs. Kuzuha, Tadashi came to town to have dinner with his mother and me.

"Kyo-chan has become a vegetarian," Mrs. Kuzuha said while we were driving to the restaurant, which she had chosen because they served some vegetarian dishes. "She doesn't eat any meat or fish. If she didn't look so healthy, I would be worried about her eating habits."

Tadashi snorted and laughed. "I'm not surprised. Kyoko, you were always such a picky eater." Mrs. Kuzuha was driving, Tadashi was in the front, and I sat in the back. Tadashi turned around in his seat and grinned at me.

"You remember my being a picky eater?" I asked.

"How can I forget? You were terrible at meals. You'd sit there picking at your food and whimpering, 'I don't want to eat this. It's bitter,' 'I don't like this because it makes a funny noise when I bite into it.' You'd complain until your mother gave up and brought you something else to eat. I used to think, 'Wow, my mother would make me sit at the table until I finished. How does she get away with being so spoiled?' "

"Yes, but you were the total opposite," I pointed out. "You could eat anything."

Tadashi laughed. I could picture him at eight or nine, cracking red boiled crab legs and sucking the meat out with a noisy slurp. His plate was piled with the empty shells of legs and bodies.

"You made fun of Jumpei for being a crybaby," he said. "But you were ten times worse at meals."

Tadashi was right. My mother was particularly indulgent in some ways. There were things she was strict about—like being considerate to our friends, showing respect to older people—but she didn't tell us not to cry or force us to eat foods we hated. She did not stress the Japanese virtue of *gaman*, "stoic perseverance." When we cried because we didn't get what we wanted or because we were mad at each other, she didn't scold us and tell us to suffer quietly. Maybe she trusted that we would stop crying on our own sooner or later. Or maybe stoic perseverance was not a virtue she particularly valued. From time to time, she called our attention to other children, grown-ups, or characters in books or movies who she thought were good examples. "See how considerate that girl is to give up her seat to that old woman on the bus?" she might say; or "Your Uncle Shiro studied very hard to become a professor" or "Your grandfather is a good teacher because he is patient." From these comments, we knew that she valued kindness, intelligence, and hard work—but she didn't seem to admire perseverance in the form of quiet suffering. When she told us to be patient, she meant being nice to other people or working hard. She wasn't telling us to shut up and suffer.

Quiet suffering was exactly what I chose, though, after her death. I gave up crying in public no matter how bad I felt, and I wrote cheerful newsy letters to my mother's family, whom my father did not allow me to see. My letters boasted about how much I enjoyed my studies, what good times my friends and I had. I now realize that no one was fooled by my stoicism.

After my father's death, Aunt Akiko was sorry that I had not had the chance to say goodbye to him or try to make peace with him. But in another way, she said, she did not feel too bad about my absence from my father's deathbed.

"Maybe it was just as well you weren't there," she told me one night when we were having tea in her kitchen. "Your father looked very bad in the last few months of his life. I didn't mind Jumpei and Kazumi seeing him like that, but you are more sensitive than they are. It would have bothered you."

Her words stunned me. Akiko knew that none of us had been close to my father—to us, seeing him sick didn't mean watching the suffering of someone we loved—and yet, she thought I was too sensitive to see my father looking bad.

What she said was the exact opposite of what I wanted to believe. I had thought of myself as the toughest of us three children since I was the oldest, the most stubborn, and the most outgoing. Kazumi and Jumpei were always nicer than I could ever be. I bullied them and made them cry when we played together as children—they never once forced me to cry or to give in and do things their way. As it turns out, Akiko had never bought my tough-guy act. She knew the truth. If I had seen my father's swollen legs or sallow face, I would have had nightmares for decades—long after Kazumi and Jumpei had forgotten. I acted the toughest and yet I was by far the biggest wimp.

In the twenty years since I left home, my life has been fairly smooth even though there were some bad times, like the last few years of graduate school. During those years, I was worried that I wouldn't be able to finish my work and even more worried that I wouldn't get a job when I finished. Getting a job didn't immediately make me happy, either: I was miserable during the first five years at my college because I didn't have time to write. Recently, going through a divorce, I cried a lot with Chuck and with a few close friends. Our breakup still makes me sad. But the bad times I had as an adult in America are completely different from the bad times I had as a teenager in Japan.

My mother's suicide singled me out as a girl without a mother. No matter how much my friends loved me, they could never understand what I was going through. I felt sealed inside my unhappiness, unable to talk about it or ask for help. I had a problem nobody could understand, in a culture where nobody was supposed to talk about personal feelings. I could see no way out of my misery. Quiet suffering was all I could choose.

During my twenties and thirties, I was not alone. I was married most of that time; Chuck and I were going through the same stages of slowly settling into the life of a full grown-up. Though neither of us liked to talk at length about how bad or scared we felt, I always knew that we were experiencing the rough transitions together. I had other friends, too. My close friends finished graduate school at the same time I did. Even after we scattered all over the country for our jobs, we stayed in touch. Last year, when I saw my friend Henri Cole at his poetry reading in Milwaukee, we reminisced about our early thirties and he said, "Those were such lean years for both of us." I felt comforted by his comment—even after we were living in separate cities, Henri in New York and me in Green Bay, Henri remembered our sharing a bad time together.

My life in Japan was miserable because I was alone and I always expected to be. When Chuck and I were going through our divorce, I didn't feel that as a divorced woman I would be all alone in the world. At least half our friends were going through the same thing. More than that, I never doubted that in spite of our divorce, Chuck and I would always have each other as good friends, as people who have shared a past. When my mother decided to die, she left me with nothing but memories I could share with no one else.

Living in the States, I am allowed to talk about painful situations and cry about them with a few friends. The bad things that happened to me after I was twenty were the same bad things that happen to many other people. I don't feel singled out by tragedy the way I used to. The platitudes people say—"Everyone has problems sometimes," "No one's life is easy"—apply to my life as an adult. I would have to be remarkably weak or petty to continue to see myself as a tragic character or a "sensitive" person. It's only natural for me to be cheerful and even-tempered now, but that is precisely what my relatives don't know. They have not known me as an adult.

When I do see my relatives, my behavior unfortunately confirms their misunderstanding that I am still a "sensitive" person. Having adopted American ways, I can't always refrain from crying if I am with people I know well and trust. For a Japanese person to cry in a private situation, even in front of family, would indicate a suffering so great as to defy politeness, self-control, perseverance, and everything she has been taught. My relatives see my tears and conclude that I must be suffering from unspeakable hurt. On the same trips when I astonish strangers by appearing "hard and dry," I alarm my family by being "wet and soft."

On my last visit to my Aunt Keiko, when I knew—and she knew too—that she was dying of cancer, I tried very hard to remain cheerful. My Uncle Kenichi and his wife, Mariko, had brought me to Keiko's house. We had sat on the floor in her Japanese-style living room for a couple of hours and talked. I was all right until the time came for us to leave. I knew that my aunt and I would never see each other again, that we were saying goodbye for the last time. Immediately, I felt the tears in the back of my eyes, and my throat got choked up. I had been sitting next to Keiko. I leaned forward and hugged her shoulder with my right hand, very lightly. Though Japanese people don't touch very much, a small hug is acceptable between women. As I pulled back, Keiko reached out and took my left hand in hers.

"You always have such a cold hand," she said, "just like your mother."

"It's a sign of a warm heart," Mariko said.

Everyone was standing up except for Keiko and me. Keiko's husband, Mr. Maeshiba, and Kenichi walked out to the hallway while Mariko lingered near the door.

"It was good to see you," I managed to say to Keiko. My voice came out like a hiccup, and tears began to leak out of my eyes. There was nothing I could do to stop crying. The harder I tried, the worse I felt.

"Be well," she said to me.

I nodded, still trying to stop crying so she wouldn't have to say a polite lie about seeing me again. I wanted her to remember me smiling and looking happy so she wouldn't have to worry about me.

"I'll be thinking of you," I said, leaning forward to give her another quick hug. She let go of my hand, I got up, waved, and walked away, afraid that I might cry harder if I didn't hurry.

"Thank you for coming to see me," she called out in her clear high voice.

I turned around and waved one last time before going out into the hallway. Everyone was outside, waiting for me by Kenichi's car. When I caught up with them, my face wet and my nose stuffed up, they all looked away, trying not to embarrass me. I knew fully that this was a gesture of their concern, respect, and love for me. They were sparing my dignity. In Wisconsin, I thought, my friends would hug me and tell me that everything would be OK—a meaningless thing to say, really—and I would cry harder for a while. I smiled and nodded at my relatives, rubbed my face with my hand, and wished that someone would hug me and tell me it was all right to cry.

Later in the car, when I had calmed down, I said that I was sorry to have cried.

"That's all right," Kenichi said. "You were always such a sensitive kid. Your mother used to worry about you."

"I'm not like that anymore," I protested, but my words sounded lame. My uncle had no reason to believe me.

"You want to listen to some music?" he asked, changing the subject.

"Sure," I answered.

Kenichi turned on the car stereo and played the sixties rock 'n' roll music my cousin Asako had taped for him. It seemed absurd to be in Japan, listening to the Rolling Stones from another era after seeing my aunt for the last time. I felt as though my whole life had been reduced to a sad anachronism, but I said nothing.

We were already a few miles away from Keiko's house. Kenichi sped up, getting ready to enter the freeway, which looked like a tangled-up concrete sculpture. As we got on the narrow, steep ramp, I took a deep breath, trying to fight off a feeling of panic. My heart was pounding, and my palms were sweaty. There was no reason to be afraid. The freeway was not as crowded as usual. I had driven through worse traffic in Chicago or Milwaukee and had never felt nervous. But I couldn't get used to how everything happened backward in Japanese traffic, the right and the left reversed. Kenichi stepped on the gas and pulled into the right lane to pass a few slower cars. Then he pulled back into the left lane, in front of the cars he had passed. To my right, across the concrete divider, a few trucks were barreling down. I was in a crazy mirror world, moving eighty miles an hour. I couldn't help imagining us in an accident, flying through the windshield or crushed against bent metal. Trying to relax, I closed my eyes. Immediately, my mind reversed the right and the left—picturing Kenichi sitting to my left and, beyond him, outside the window, the empty passing lane. It was an old reflex. I wanted to feel safe. I couldn't help trying to imagine that everything was where I wanted it to be.

The summer I worked as a volunteer songbird rehabilitator in Green Bay, many of my friends told me that they would never be able to do the same work because they were too emotional. They would get too attached to the birds they cared for and have to cry every time one of them died. They said I must be a brave person to take on a big responsibility that could end up in heartbreak.

I didn't think my work required courage—all I had to do was be sensible. From the beginning, I knew that some of the birds I tried to save would die. Even regular birds succeed in raising only about half their young, so babies who fall out of the nest at two or three days old are doomed to die. Any minute they lived in my care was an extra minute they wouldn't have lived, so I had no reason to cry when they died. Most of the birds I took home were a little older; they survived and were ready for release in a month or so. Release was a task some people found difficult—after spending so much time with the bird, you have to let it go, to live or die in the wild as it was meant to—but I liked doing it. I loved opening the door of my outdoor cage and watching the finches and waxwings fly out, swirling up into the sky without looking back once at me. Some of the robins stayed around in our yard for a few weeks, begging food from me, but even they left to join the other birds.

In mid-August, someone brought in a baby nighthawk, and the curator, Mike, gave it to me. Nighthawks, unlike most songbirds, don't gape for their food. They come running at you, whistling and hissing, flapping their wings, opening and closing their mouths very fast. You have to have perfect timing to put food in their mouths. Because the birds are nocturnal, they don't start flying around during the day, as other birds do; nor do they perch on branches—their feet are made for staying on big flat surfaces. I spent more time and care on this bird than on the others, trying to teach him to fly and eat. After three weeks, I noticed that the nighthawk's beak was slightly crooked and his mouth did not close tightly. Mike arranged for me to take the bird to a veterinarian in town.

After examining the bird, the veterinarian told me that he had most likely suffered some traumatic injury when he fell out of the nest, and as a result, his beak would never develop properly.

"This is a bird that has to fly around at night. He flies with his mouth open, and moths and mosquitoes get trapped inside his mouth. Your bird is not going to be able to do that with this deformed beak."

"What can we do?" I asked, thinking that there must be some corrective surgery or even braces we could use—I had seen all kinds of injured birds nursed to health.

The veterinarian shook her head. "I'm sorry to have to tell

you this, but there's nothing we can do for this little guy. Nighthawks don't do well in captivity. The only fair thing to do is to put him down."

"OK," I said, though I was stunned. "Are you going to do that?"

"No," she said. "Our arrangement with the sanctuary is that they have to use their own facility for euthanasia. I only volunteer my time for examinations."

"So I should take the bird back to the sanctuary and talk to Mike, and he'll take care of the rest."

She nodded.

I put the bird in the carrier, got in my car, and shut the door. Immediately, the bird began whistling and hissing and running toward me. Even from inside the carrier, he could see me. That bird recognized me as his caretaker. Birds can distinguish between one person and another. The robins that had stayed in our yard flew down from their perch when they saw me and begged for worms, but they paid no attention to Chuck or my neighbors. The nighthawk, too, knew me. I began to feel pretty bad.

It was a fifteen-minute drive from the veterinarian's to the sanctuary. I pulled over twice on the shoulder because I was crying too hard to drive. I thought of calling my friend Diane from a pay phone and asking her to take the bird to the sanctuary—I knew she would do that for me, but then she would have to feel bad about the bird. I pulled myself together and drove into the sanctuary, parked my car, picked up the carrier, and headed for Mike's office. I kept my sunglasses on so no one would see my red eyes.

I had forgotten that it was Thursday, the day some of the volunteers and interns got together for their weekly potluck lunch in the big room next to Mike's office. A dozen people were sitting down around the table eating. There were salads and casseroles and loaves of bread.

"Hi, how did it go with the nighthawk?" one of the interns, Maureen, asked me.

"Not so great," I said. My voice came out wrong.

"What's the matter?" Maureen asked, standing up from the chair where she had been eating. "Are you all right?"

A few other people stood up quickly and walked toward me. I put the carrier on the floor, took off my sunglasses, and started to cry. I had gone past the point where I could stop and pretend that this was not happening. There was nothing to do now except to keep on crying.

"Where's Mike?" I asked, barely able to speak. "The nighthawk has to be put down because his beak isn't right. I need to talk to Mike."

"I'll go get him," someone said, and I heard her leaving.

In the meantime, Maureen had put her arms around me, another woman was handing me some paper towels—apologizing that she couldn't find any Kleenex—and a couple of other people were surrounding me, all looking very concerned. I knew everyone there from the training sessions we had attended together, but except for Maureen, whom I saw almost every day when I came to pick up a new bird to care for, I didn't know them that well. I blew my nose and got myself under control, feeling stupid and embarrassed.

One of the women said, "Hey, sit down. Help yourself to some food."

I turned toward her, and I'm sure I looked none too grateful. *What is she talking about?* I thought. *Why would I want to eat? I'm upset, not hungry.*

"Really," she insisted. "Here, have this piece of cake."

"No, thanks," I said, as politely as I could manage. The sight of the cake—a yellow sheet cake with pink frosting—made me sick. Eating is the last thing I want to do when I'm upset and can hardly breathe. "I'm not hungry."

"Well," the woman said, "if you change your mind, here are the plates." She pointed to the stack of plastic plates.

"Thanks," I said, still sniffling a little.

When Mike came back, I went into his office and told him what the veterinarian had said. I'm sure he could see that I had been crying. He handed me some more paper towels, and I managed to listen to his explanations—he agreed with the veterinarian—without further tears.

"Why don't you just leave the carrier here?" he said when we were done talking. He had taken the bird out to look at the beak himself. Now he was absent-mindedly petting its feathers. "I'll take care of this." I knew he had to put the bird in the carrier and take him to the other building, where they euthanized animals.

I was grateful that Mike was letting me leave with some semblance of dignity. I walked out the door, through the big room where people were still eating. Most of them looked at me in silence—in such a way that I knew they were sorry for me—but the woman who had offered me the cake said, "Look, if you want to talk about it, I'll be home tonight. My number's in the phone book."

"All right, thanks," I said, and walked back to the car.

The woman who offered me the food meant well, but I had no intention of calling her: I scarcely knew her and didn't want to discuss my feelings with her. After wishing that my Japanese relatives would give me a hug and acknowledge my tears, I was wishing that this woman had left me alone and saved my dignity. I was completely inconsistent, but I didn't care.

All that afternoon, I could think of nothing else. My own feelings scared me. When I went into the outdoor cage in my yard to feed the waxwings and robins that were still left, I felt sad remembering how the nighthawk used to sit on the log on the ground, making a faint whistling noise and blinking his eyes. I had been fooling myself all summer, when I thought I was so much tougher than my friends, so much more reasonable. That wasn't true at all. I had felt a strong attachment, even a crazy kind of love for that nighthawk. I loved the way he would sit on the palm of my hand as I held out my arm at shoulder-height. Slowly, I would lower my hand, making him open and flap his large wings that had a bright white spot. I was training him to use the muscles he needed for flight. I wanted to release him some late summer night; I would launch him on his first all-night flying feast, and he would go away free but remembering me in a small corner of his brain. There was nothing rational about my attachment to that bird.

As the waxwings and robins crowded around me in the cage, all of them screaming to be fed, I wasn't sure if I should continue caring for them. I had enjoyed my work because I thought the whole process proved that I was capable of both devotion and detachment: I could act like an anxious and overprotective mother for a few weeks and then let the birds go without regret because I respected their independence. In a small way, I thought, I was practicing an ideal kind of love, caring but rational, devoted but not possessive. After I cried about the nighthawk, I was forced to admit—yet again—that there is nothing rational about love and devotion. I didn't like that realization at all.

For a few days, my eyes would get wet every time I thought of the nighthawk. Watching the robins splash around in their birdbath, I didn't laugh at their antics. Wet birds looked so pathetic. Going into the bird cage gave me a helpless and vulnerable feeling. I didn't talk about my feelings with anyone. I didn't even want to think about them too much. In the end, I got over my sadness because time passed and I learned to ignore it.

That's the only way I know to get over the strong feelings that scare me. When I lose something or somebody, whether it is a friend who has to move far away or an animal that dies, losing them seems to bring me back, temporarily, to feeling like a helpless child. The only way I can deal with the panic and desolation that comes with loss is to learn to ignore it. I practice the Japanese way of stoic perseverance and denial.

In most situations, I am a big believer in acknowledging and talking about painful issues and dealing with them step by step. At different times in my life, I saw therapists and found them very helpful. I agree with them that talking is the first step to understanding and overcoming the negative events in our lives. But there are just a few things I don't ever expect to understand or overcome. The panic I feel about loss, the fear I have about dying, the love I feel for people or animals who are doomed to leave me—these feelings belong in that category. With feelings like these, talking doesn't do any good. I already know that my feelings are irrational. There is nothing more to understand. All I can do, to go on, is to treat these feelings as aberrations from my otherwise smooth life—to politely and stoically ignore them in the way I was brought up to do. None of us can reason our way out of terrible fear or despair, any more than we can reason our way into faith and hope. But there comes a moment when I can will myself to stop thinking about the feelings that terrify me. It's like turning off a switch. The harsh light that was glaring in my face simply goes off, and that is that.

After the nighthawk had to be put down, I took in several more birds, and a few of them died. The sanctuary had a policy that if an animal died in our care, we had to bring in the body. We worked with the Department of Natural Resources, and they wanted everything accounted for. A few weeks after I cried in front of everyone, I had to bring in the body of a chipping sparrow. I had expected the bird to die— it had crashed into a windowpane and smashed its head. The bird was in my care for only a day before it died.

I drove in with the bird in a small plastic bag and handed it to Mike, who was outside repairing a hole in one of the cages.

"The chipping sparrow died. You know, the one with the head injury."

Immediately, he looked up from what he was doing. The way he was frowning but trying to smile, I knew he was worried about me.

"Don't worry about it," I assured him. "I'm not stressed

about this in any way. I knew this bird was going to die. I'm not going to start crying or anything."

"OK," he said, smiling.

"I want to apologize for what happened the other day," I said. "I don't make a habit of crying in front of people. I'm not going to be weird about dead birds. I'm not like that. I only cry three times a year, if that."

"Oh, I'm sure I cry more often than that, myself," Mike said. "I'm not worried about you." Mike examined the dead sparrow, turning the plastic bag around in his hand. "Yeah," he said, "most of these birds that hit windows, if they don't get up and fly away right away, they usually end up dead."

I nodded, updated him about the other birds still in my care, and left. I was touched by what Mike said about crying more often than I did, even though it was probably a polite lie to save my pride. After telling me that he wasn't worried about me, he had tactfully changed the subject and talked business, so we didn't have to dwell on what was a painful and embarrassing recollection for me. I felt good about our conversation. For once, someone had found a happy medium between acknowledging my tears and saving my dignity.

Since that summer, I have not cried in front of a group of near-strangers, and I would like to keep it that way. Only a few close friends have seen my tears, and not that often. Tears do have some positive associations. "Teardrop shape" is a delicate shape—the shape of gems or cut glass. Tears taste salty, like the sea, like the beginning of life. But crying is an awkward and unromantic experience and there is no getting around that. In novels or movies, beautiful heroines may shed beautiful tears, but our real-life experience is nothing like that: choked up, we breathe noisily and eventually have to blow our noses. Nobody looks good while crying. Most of us look almost comical with our red eyes and flattened hair, a crumpled handkerchief or tissue clutched in our hands.

Sometimes, when I feel like crying, I remember what my mother used to say to make me laugh—a Japanese saying she repeated because it sounded funny: *sakki naita karasu ga mo warau*. It meant, "The crow that was crying a few minutes ago is already laughing now." My mother didn't have to scold my brother and me for crying or encourage us to be stoic, because she could usually make us laugh. When she repeated this saying, I imagined the three of us—my mother, brother, and me—turning into big black birds flapping our wings and screaming. I laughed, picturing us perched on trees and cawing. If we were crows, I thought, no one would know if we were laughing or crying.

This was my mother's gift. Crows are smart and stubborn. They are tough birds that survive and wheel around in the sky on their big wings. My mother wanted us to imagine ourselves flying around, making a racket, and laughing-crying-singing. In Japanese, the word for crying, *naku*, also means "birds making noise," although the two verbs are written with different pictorial characters. In conversation, the two words sound exactly the same: a flock of blackbirds rise up to the sky, leaving us with the clamor of their singing and crying.

LIES

❋

The hardest part of my job as a teacher is getting people to tell the truth.

"I liked your story a lot," my students say to one another during the peer critique sessions of our creative writing classes. "I thought it was very good."

Later, in my office, they often confide, "I didn't like that story at all. The plot was trite and predictable. The dialogue was bad. People talked like they were characters from a soap opera."

I don't know how to bridge the gap between the polite lies people tell one another and the harsh criticisms they make in private. What I want is something between these two extremes: courteous and constructive criticism. That's the hardest thing for my students to give—or for me to encourage—because all of us have been trained since childhood to tell polite lies to save other people's feelings.

"Don't be personal and negative," we've been taught. "If you don't have something nice to say, don't say anything."

The format I use for our writing workshops reinforces our polite habits. I ask the students to start the peer critique sessions with what they liked about the story, what they considered to be its strengths. After a few minutes, I reiterate the "strengths" people have pointed out, and only then do I feel ready to ask, "Is there anything in the story that you were confused by? Any parts you felt should have been developed more or cut out? Anything you might do differently if it were your story?" My questions are answered at first with a few tentative comments; but after the ice is broken, almost everyone pitches in, offering opinions in animated (though polite) conversations. Our discussion follows the same polite pattern we use to criticize others—starting with, "I like So-and-so and we get along, but . . ."

This is the standard format that many writing teachers use, and it isn't necessarily bad. It sets a friendly tone. Having agreed that the story has merits, the class feels less inhibited about pointing out the few things that need improvement, and the writer can hear the criticism without feeling personally attacked. But the scenario does not work well when we discuss stories that need more than a little improvement. After spending the first few minutes on the story's supposed strengths, nobody feels ready to admit, "I'm afraid that the whole concept is wrong. Maybe you should put this story aside and do something different." Unfortunately, that is sometimes the only honest thing we can say.

Every semester, a few students write stories that won't improve through revision because the whole premise is wrong: a story about "justice" that takes place in a court-room even though the writer has never witnessed a trial; a story at the end of which we realize that the narrator is a dog; a story that is a "dialogue" between Satan and God; that sort of thing. I try to prevent these stories from getting workshopped in class. In my private conference with the student, I tell the truth: "You would be better off writing something else, because this story doesn't quite work out. Why don't you put your energies into a different story? Don't revise this one. Just start over and do something else." Most people are willing to take my advice, but for the few who won't, I don't have a policy that would allow me, the instructor, to bar anyone's work from classroom discussion. So the stubborn few students end up workshopping their stories and feeling encouraged by everyone's polite remarks. Theirs are the stories that occasion some of the other students to come to me with the truth: "Actually, I didn't like that story."

"Why didn't you say that in class?" I ask.

The answer is usually the same: "I didn't want to be too negative."

I sympathize with my students when they can't bring themselves to be honest. I have the same problem. I tell the truth to my students because that is my job, but in every other situation, I am as politely dishonest as anyone.

"I liked your poems," I often say to people who send me the poems they wrote to overcome some tragedy in their lives. "I could see that writing helped you a lot." In private, I might value the poems as a form of therapy but not as works of art. But except to people who are officially my students (or former students or writer friends with whom I have a mutually honest relationship), I won't have the courage to say, "I'm glad you found writing to be a helpful activity, but as poems, these don't work." I know that every time I don't tell the truth, I am compromising the truths I do tell. If I don't tell people when I think something is bad, how can they take me seriously when I say and mean that their work is good?

I would like to believe that my failure to be honest is a sign of consideration or kindness: I care about others and don't want to hurt their feelings. But that is simply not the case. I don't find it any easier to tell unpleasant truths to people I don't know or don't like. I tell lies because I want to spare myself the embarrassment of appearing negative and unpleasant: I want to protect myself as well as—or more than—the other person.

Not a week goes by without my telling a lie, but I suppose that is the same for most people. The polite but untrue compliments we offer can be dismissed as "white lies"—small lies we tell to protect ourselves and/or others from trouble or embarrassment. I am not sure how small or harmless any lie is, but if there is any justification for white lies, it is that they are usually expressions of what we wish were the truth. When I lie to people about liking their poems, their new haircuts, or the gifts they gave me, I wish that what I am saying were the truth. If I tell a friend that I missed the party at her house because I was tired and didn't feel well—rather than because I didn't feel enthusiastic about going in the first place—I am half convinced, myself, that I really was feeling a little under the weather that night. What I say is an extension, rather than a contradiction, of the truth—something that could easily have been so. Perhaps in resorting to these lies, we are only telling our friends what they, too, wish were the truth.

Most of us fall into the habit of wishful lying. Sometimes, if we are lucky, we can even make our lies become the truth. After lying to a friend about not being able to come to her party because we planned to be out of town, we can actually go out of town to make the lie "come true." In Japan, white lies are widely accepted—even encouraged. From an early age, we are taught that there is a distinction between hon-ne (the truth, literally, the true-sound) and tate-mae (the polite lie, or the façade). Everyone lies from time to time, we are told; it's naive and even rude to expect otherwise. In the States, sincerity and honesty are ideals, but most people admit to falling short of them. Most Americans believe that there is a big difference between being viciously insincere and being insincere with good intentions or out of politeness. Whatever the ideals and the codes of behavior may be in the two cultures, the result is pretty much the same: we all lie to avoid mutual embarrassment, to save face.

As a teenager in Japan, I did not value the custom of hon-ne/tate-mae. To be insincere, I thought, was the worst offense. My favorite characters in literature were Jane Eyre and Holden Caulfield. I admired their righteous indignation about hypocrisy and phoniness. It didn't bother me that Holden lied occasionally—his lies got him into deeper trouble rather than giving him an advantage, and besides, he was honest with us, the readers. Trying to be as pure-minded as Jane Eyre, I went out of my way to tell and insist on unpopular truths. I flaunted my disobedience to my father and my stepmother. I confronted my friends with the mistakes they made, the stupid things they said. It's a wonder that anyone could stand me at all.

Ironically, during this time when I worshipped the truth, I was being fed some big lies by my stepmother. I believed all Michiko's lies because she was such an unpleasant person. To me, liars were people who pretended to be nice, whose sweet words and malicious actions didn't match. Michiko never tried to be nice to me, spare my feelings, or save my face, so I assumed that she was being truthful to me. I even thought that blunt honesty was one of her few good qualities. I couldn't have been more wrong. The whole time we lived together, she was actually trying to isolate me from anyone who could have made me feel loved or valued, and her strategy almost always involved lies.

Even before she moved into our house, Michiko told my father that my mother's family had made her feel uncomfortable; she couldn't really be any sort of a "mother" to my brother and me unless we stopped seeing them. My father agreed, but I was still allowed to see Akiko and Kazumi since Akiko was my father's sister, not my mother's. I visited them every Sunday and spent my afternoons at their house. When Michiko told me that I was bothering Akiko by spending too much time at her house, I was shocked, but it never occurred to me that she was lying.

"Akiko wants to spend her Sundays alone with Kazumi," Michiko explained. "After all, Kazumi is her daughter and you are only a niece."

In Japan, when people are forced to communicate something painful or unpleasant, they use a middle-person, so I assumed that Akiko did not have the heart to tell me "the truth" and had asked Michiko to be her messenger. I stopped visiting Akiko and Kazumi and never thought of confronting them or telling them how hurt I felt.

I was thirteen then and no longer in touch with many people from my childhood. None of my friends at school had met my mother or known me as a girl who had a mother. My family had moved to a new house, so I didn't play with kids from our old neighborhood. The only people I still knew from my old life were the Kuzuhas, our former neighbors, who now lived a few miles away. My father couldn't forbid me to see them, since he and Mr. Kuzuha worked at the same office.

For several years after my mother's death, Mrs. Kuzuha invited me to her house every week to have dinner with her and her sons or to go on various outings with them. Some Saturdays, she took me shopping alone, leaving her sons at home, since they were not interested in looking at women's clothes or shoes. Mrs. Kuzuha said that I was like a daughter to her, and I, too, felt that she was like a mother to me. Unlike Jumpei, Makoto and Tadashi remembered my mother and talked about her now and then, so they were more like my brothers than my real brother. Mr. Kuzuha, who watched television at home on Sundays or took the boys and me to the park, was so much nicer than my own father. He joked and teased me as my uncles used to. When I was with the Kuzuhas, I felt as though I still had a family. I didn't know that Michiko was calculating how to separate me from them with her lies.

She had her chance one evening when I was sixteen, when Mrs. Kuzuha took me out to dinner in Osaka. By then, Makoto was attending a boarding school in Tokyo and

Tadashi had too much homework, but she brought along Makoto's roommate, who happened to be staying at her house for a few days. At the end of the evening, she asked the roommate to walk me home from the commuter train station because it was late and she did not want me to walk or take a cab alone. "I just want Kyo-chan to be safe," she said. "I can't come along because I can't walk in these high heels."

The boy and I assured her that we would be safe and told her not to worry. When the two of us got back to my house, though, my father had been looking out the window, waiting for me. As soon as he saw me with a boy, Hiroshi assumed that I had lied to him about going out to dinner with Mrs. Kuzuha—all along, he thought, I was dating a boy in secret. He came running out and started yelling at us. I asked the boy to leave. "You're only making it worse," I said. "Go."

The next day, I called Mrs. Kuzuha from school because I felt mortified by my father's behavior. She told me it wasn't my fault, and I thought that was the end of the incident.

When I got home, Michiko came running to the door to meet me. "You won't believe what happened this afternoon," she said, standing in the hallway with a dirty dishrag in her hand. "Mrs. Kuzuha called and she is furious with all of us."

"What?" I asked, confused. Michiko had not given me time to take off my shoes or put down my books.

"Mrs. Kuzuha was upset at your father for yelling at her son's friend, but she wasn't too happy with you, either," Michiko said, breathless with excitement. "Mrs. Kuzuha thinks that you aren't such a nice girl anymore. 'Kyoko is changing,' she told me. 'She's taken to flirting with boys. I've caught her making eyes at my own sons.' " Michiko snorted through her nose as though she were upset. "Mrs. Kuzuha then accused me of not being a good parent. She kept saying that you used to be such a nice girl and now you aren't because I must not be doing a good job."

Michiko went on about all the bad things Mrs. Kuzuha had said about me. I stood there in shock. I had no idea then that Michiko had made up the conversation she was reporting, though I know now that Mrs. Kuzuha only called to say that I hadn't been lying to my parents, that I really had been out with her. Michiko invented everything else. But back then, I assumed that she was telling me an unpleasant truth. After she was finished, I went upstairs and cried. I felt angry at Michiko for the apparent pleasure she took in reporting the conversation she'd had, but I was angry at Mrs. Kuzuha, too, for pretending to be so nice when she had such a low opinion of me.

I saw the Kuzuhas only a few more times after that day. Mrs. Kuzuha continued to call me and invite me to her house. When I couldn't come up with a good excuse and went there, she was friendly and kind. There was no sign that she thought of me as "not a nice girl anymore," but I concluded that Mrs. Kuzuha was an expert pretender—a hypocrite.

The following spring, I left to spend a year in Arizona as an AFS student. I didn't write to the Kuzuhas; I didn't contact them when I got back. In two years, I was gone again for good. I never tried to get in touch with the Kuzuhas again.

From time to time, though, I thought about Tadashi and

Makoto. They appeared in my dreams, as children or teen-agers or even as grown-ups. When I saw my father in 1990, I asked him if he ever ran into any of the Kuzuhas or heard any news of them.

"No," he replied. "I never hear anything about them."

I was in Kobe for eight weeks that summer. I looked in the phone book and found out that Mr. and Mrs. Kuzuha still lived in Ashiya. I thought of calling them, but I kept putting it off until it was too late. I didn't know what I could say to them after all those years.

When I was in town after my father's death, I looked up the Kuzuhas' phone number again. This time, I called. Mrs. Kuzuha answered and said that she had heard the news of my father's death, that her husband had also died the year be-fore.

"Can you come to visit me?" she asked. "I'll come and get you in my car. We should have dinner."

"Of course," I said.

As soon as I met Mrs. Kuzuha in her car, I knew that she had never said a bad thing about me. She turned to me, put her hand on my cheek as though I were still a little girl, and cried. I realized how ridiculous I had been to believe that she would complain to Michiko—a woman she never liked—about me, a girl she had known for years, a girl whose mother had been her best friend.

During our dinner at her house, Mrs. Kuzuha mentioned that she had run into my father at a restaurant in the early eighties when Makoto was working in Chicago. She asked him where I was, and my father did not tell her. "Makoto is in Chicago right now," she told him. "He would love to get in touch with Kyoko. I heard a rumor that she, too, was in the Midwest.''

''Yes, she is,'' my father answered but would not tell her where. When Mrs. Kuzuha asked for my address, my father walked away from her.

''Makoto looked in the phone books of all the major cities in the Midwest, but he couldn't find you,'' Mrs. Kuzuha told me.

I had been in Milwaukee at the time, but my phone number wasn't listed. I was disappointed to learn—years too late—that Makoto and I had been within two hours' drive of each other.

I called Tadashi from Mrs. Kuzuha's house, and he, too, said that he had run into my father once in the mid-eighties and had talked to him briefly.

When my father told me, in 1990, that he hadn't heard a thing about the Kuzuhas, he had actually seen both Mrs. Kuzuha and Tadashi not so long ago. I was angry that he had been rude to them and then lied to me.

When I came home from Mrs. Kuzuha's house, I told my aunt what I had found out.

''Why would my father say nothing about meeting the Kuzuhas when I specifically asked him about them?'' I asked, more or less rhetorically.

Instead of agreeing with me that my father's behavior was odd or wrong, Akiko frowned and shook her head. We were having tea in her kitchen. She put down her cup and shrugged.

''I don't know why your father was rude, but in a way, I understand. Mrs. Kuzuha hasn't always been fair to you,'' she said. ''Your father told me what happened.'' She proceeded to tell me a story about myself that amazed me.

According to my father—who heard it from Michiko—
when I was sixteen I wrote numerous love letters to Makoto's
roommate who had walked me home that one night. Over
and over, I begged the boy to visit me. The roommate's
family discovered the letters and got very upset—they asked
the Kuzuhas to make me stop. Mrs. Kuzuha, caught in the
middle of an awkward situation, was angry at me. She called
our house and yelled at Michiko and blamed her for not
having kept a better eye on me. Michiko had to talk to me
and make me promise that I would never write, telephone,
or try to see this boy.

When Akiko finished her story, I was too astonished to
speak for a while. The story sounded so completely authentic
even though I knew it to be a total fabrication. How could I
defend myself against such a good story? "But I never wrote
any letters" was all I could say right away.

"You didn't?" Akiko asked, looking surprised.

"I can't even remember that boy's name," I told her. "I
only met him that one time with Mrs. Kuzuha and never
thought of him."

My aunt frowned. "You never even sent him one post-
card?"

"Why would I? I had nothing to say to him. Think about
it, Aunt Akiko. Why would I write love letters to a boy I only
met once? Especially when that boy was Makoto's roommate.
How embarrassing."

"I did think it was odd," Akiko admitted. "I was a little
surprised when your father told me."

"Believe me. I never even thought about that boy, much
less wrote to him."

"I believe you," Akiko said, frowning and nodding at the
same time. "I feel bad now that I was so foolish."

"Don't blame yourself, Aunt Akiko. Michiko is a pretty good liar."

Akiko and I couldn't get over Michiko's skill at deception. To me, Michiko had reported a single fictional conversation with Mrs. Kuzuha. Maybe that wasn't so hard. But to my father, she had concocted a long story about my love letters, their discovery, and Mrs. Kuzuha's complaints. She must have also told him about an invented conversation she and I had had, in which she made me promise not to write to the boy anymore. She would have had to make up details about how I had been forced to admit "the truth" about the letters, how I had cried when she confronted me. "There's no need for you to say anything," she must have told my father. "It's all taken care of. I told her that in return for her promise, I would make sure no one else would ever mention this embarrassing event to her again. So you should say nothing. I only told you all these unpleasant details so you would know the whole truth. After all, you are her father."

I'm still amazed at her confidence. If my father had made even a slight reference to the supposed love letters, I would have said, "What love letters? What are you talking about?"

But as Michiko would have known by that time, my father always assumed the worst about me. He wasn't the kind of father who would have thought, "Maybe there was some misunderstanding. I want to hear my daughter's side of the story," or "If my daughter wants to write to someone, she has every right to do so. It's no one else's business." My father was probably relieved that he would not have to talk to me about this—or anything else. He must have seen the whole incident as another example of how I made him and our family look bad. He snubbed Mrs. Kuzuha at the restaurant and refused to give her my address because he was angry at her for the part he thought she had played in adding to our humiliation. It didn't occur to him that a woman who was my mother's best friend might have defended me if I had been found in the middle of an embarrassing situation. Like me, my father believed everything Michiko said.

Michiko hasn't changed. She continues to tell stories that show everyone but herself in a bad light. I am sure that I am still a subject of her wild tales, but I don't confront her with her lies because it is useless. No matter what I say, she will make up more lies. Maybe in some crazy way, she is convinced by now that I really did write love letters to Makoto's roommate, that no one in this world is as virtuous or as put-upon by others as is she.

A few months ago, I was looking through the *Joy of Cooking* to find a recipe for a cookie frosting. I thumbed through the book instead of using the index and found myself browsing in the Game section. On the first page of that section, there were drawings of rabbits and squirrels. The one that caught my eye showed a stylishly laced-up boot placed firmly on a squirrel's tail while two gloved hands pulled up the legs. The drawing went with the instructions for skinning a squirrel:

ABOUT SQUIRREL Gray squirrels are the preferred ones; red squirrels are small and quite gamey in flavor. There are, proverbially, many ways to skin a squirrel, but some hunters claim the following one is the quickest and cleanest. It needs a sharp knife.

"Hey, look at this," I called to the friend whose book it was. "Did you know your book had these helpful instructions about cooking squirrels?"

We read the rest of the instructions and laughed in the way we would laugh at anything that was "sick" or "gross." My friend, who grew up in rural Wisconsin, admitted that he had eaten squirrels in the past when his grandmother put on an annual "squirrel feed," but no, he had never skinned or cleaned them himself. I wanted to know all about what they tasted like and how they were served. "They didn't taste like chicken, did they?" I asked.

"No, they tasted kind of gamy," he said.

"What does that mean anyway, gamy? That's no more specific than saying that something 'tastes like chicken.' Does that mean sweet, bitter, sour, or what?"

"I don't know," he said, shaking his head. "For someone who doesn't eat meat, you're kind of fascinated by all this."

I couldn't stop asking about all the gory details. I learned that at my friend's grandmother's house, squirrels were served with their heads, tails, and feet cut off, looking like "squirrel chassis." I liked that expression because it sounded almost surreal—a Salvador Dali combination of the natural and the mechanical. For weeks, I kept telling everyone who had the Joy of Cooking to look at page 453.

What is repulsive is often fascinating, especially if it's detailed. The squirrel picture would have been less interesting if the boot placed on the tail had been a workboot, like the Sorels that many Midwesterners wear in the winter. The delicate shape of the low-heeled but slim boot—unmistakably a "ladies'" boot—made the picture memorable. I wondered if the artist had chosen that boot to communicate to the readers—most of them women—that they did not need a man in order to cook squirrels. At the same time, the instructions mentioned "hunters," making it sound like certain people hunted squirrels as a way of life. All of those details interested me very much.

I find Michiko's lies fascinating and repulsive in a similar way. Even in my anger, I could not help but wonder exactly what she must have said to my father to prevent him from confronting me about the supposed love letters. I wanted to know the details of her lies and her thinking—just as I wanted to know what "gamy" really meant.

The lies Michiko told are nothing like the white lies most people tell, wishfully exaggerating the truth. Hers involve making up—from scratch, as it were—a series of circumstances, facts, and details. I still wonder what motivated Michiko to choose the particular scenario about my writing love letters, just as I wonder what motivated the *Joy of Cooking* illustrator to choose a particular boot as the instrument of squirrel-skinning.

Lies are fascinating because there are so many possibilities for invention and embellishment. In a liar's mouth, facts are no longer boring and predictable, but interesting and surprising. The sense of unlimited possibility is what lies have in common with another vice that most people find irresistible: gossip. Gossip is interesting because what we hear and pass on to others may be the truth, but it could also be a wild fantasy; we are captivated by the very uncertainty of what we hear.

In spite of the proverb, the truth is seldom as strange or

interesting as fiction. Most of us don't want to know the painful facts about other people's lives. I often feel burdened when friends confide in me about their marriage problems, childhood traumas, or job dissatisfactions. Even though I try my best to console and reassure, I can't help wishing—selfishly—that my friends had told someone else. Most people feel the same way: hearing a confidence is a duty. When someone is a good confidante, we see that person as possessing a virtue.

Gossip is entirely different. There is nothing virtuous about engaging in gossip, but we enjoy it to the utmost. When someone tells us vague rumors about someone else's marriage problems, childhood secrets, or job scandals, our ears prick up. When the same information is told to us in confidence, we feel a sinking sense of duty. We listen silently and carefully, trying to think of the few right words to say and maybe getting a headache in the process. When the information is passed on to us as gossip, we jump into the conversation with gusto: nobody knows the truth anyway, so we are free to offer our own theories, conjectures, and interpretations. We can talk all we want.

To gossip is to "talk behind someone's back," to be sneaky, to take liberties. But the guilt I feel about gossiping is similar to the guilt I feel about speeding on the freeway or bringing my own food into movie theaters instead of buying popcorn at the concession stand: the guilt never cancels out my pleasure in getting away with the offense. Gossip can be malicious. It can be used to spread false rumors, to destroy someone's reputation, but most of the time, people who gossip don't intend to do any of this.

My friends and I like to gossip because gossip is a sort of free-for-all talk-a-thon. Sitting around with cups of coffee, we can spend the whole afternoon offering various theories and interpretations about what might "really be going on" in someone's marriage or why two people we work with seem to hate each other. Our interpretations and theories are usually kind or neutral. Maybe we stretch the few facts we know and try to outdo one another with our imaginings and perceptions, but we don't assume the worst about the people we are talking about. Usually, all we feel toward them is a mild good wish. We conclude many of our statements with, "Well, I hope everything works out for them," "We'll see what happens next week," "I'm sure they'll come through this crisis and be just fine." We don't care what will really happen in the future: the main pleasure of gossip is talk, not the subject, the outcome, or the information. If, after two hours of conversation, none of us knows anything we didn't already know at the start, we aren't disappointed at all. It's like when we go shopping and nobody buys anything after four hours—who cares? We spent time together and talked; what more could we want?

The emphasis on talking—talking for talking's sake—may be what divides men and women in the matter of gossip. The way we gossip could be one of the few real differences between us. The "manly" ideals of "being fair" and not getting "too personal" about other people seem to affect all my male friends. Even the few men I gossip with—who are not traditional "macho" types by any means—do not gossip with other men in the same way they do with me.

If "gossip" meant simply talking about other people in their absence, men could be said to gossip as much as women. Just like women, men talk about people they work with, comparing stories about whether the new principal or supervisor is a good administrator. They offer their interpre-

tations about their colleagues: "Is he comfortable with people?" "Is she organized?" "Does his secretary like working
with him?" But when I go out for drinks with my colleagues, most of whom are men, and we talk about people
who are not there, I am struck by how little the conversation
strays from immediate facts and evidence. So-and-so did this
or said that; therefore, he must be insecure with people. So-
and-so drives this kind of car; therefore, he must like to
show off. Nobody says, "I wonder what So-and-so's father
was like?" or "Is he an only child or does he come from a
big family?" The few times I brought up such questions—
questions any woman would ask right away—men looked at
me with a big frown as if to say, "What? Why are you talking about that?" My speculations were too personal and yet
too removed from the immediate circumstance and the "evidence" before us. It was unfair and petty to talk about someone's family or upbringing (but not his car); the past was
irrelevant.

What my women friends and I could spend three hours
talking about and not resolving in the end can be dispatched,
with something like the "answer," in ten minutes of male
conversation. Men don't talk just to talk; they talk to exchange information or to solve a problem. When they offer
theories or make predictions, they are concerned about the
accuracy of their words. They end their discussion with
"We'll see what happens next week" because it's only fair to
be cautious, to add a disclaimer to the prediction they just
made. For me and my women friends, "We'll see what happens" means "I really don't have any idea what will happen,
but I enjoyed talking about this. Now it's your turn."

Men make little distinction in their conversations between
people they know and those they don't. They discuss profes-

sional athletes, presidential candidates, or musicians in the way women would talk about people who live across the street. The way men talk about them, public figures don't sound like faraway people, because so many facts and details are known about them—batting averages, places of origin, former coaches, slumps and good seasons, scandals and awards, who played backup on whose album ten years ago. "So-and-so just resigned (or was fired)," my male friends say to one another about a basketball coach in California—with as much shock or disappointment as they might express if the same thing were to happen to the associate dean of academic affairs at our college. Their tone suggests a conversation about a mutual friend, not someone they have and will never meet.

Women engage in impersonal gossip, too, about movie stars and other famous people—the checkout counters of grocery stores are crowded with "gossip" magazines marketed for women. But the women who read those magazines don't talk about Madonna and Elizabeth Taylor in the same familiar tone men use to talk about athletes and rock musicians. Madonna and Elizabeth Taylor are fascinating because their lives are so removed from ours—to most of us, they may as well be figments of our imagination. We don't feel intimacy or familiarity toward them regardless of how many personal facts we know about them. Nobody expects the *National Enquirer* or the *Star* to stick to the facts; "gossip" magazines can entice their readers precisely because they contain exaggerations and wild guesses. Magazines marketed for men highlight facts, whether they are football statistics, stereo product information, or profiles of successful business people.

Our attitudes toward public figures mirror our attitudes

toward gossip in general: women like to talk, speculating about what may or may not be true, whereas men like to trade "inside information" based on facts. Women have a different tone or level of intimacy for talking about people they know personally, as opposed to talking about famous strangers, but that is not true for men. If anything, men seem more intimate, less inhibited, when they talk about public figures.

But information isn't everything even for men. My male friends often reminisce together about their favorite rock groups from the sixties or the football stars they worshiped when they were seven. That is their way of talking about a common childhood—miles, states, or continents apart, they were listening to the same music and watching the same games on TV. When men talk about the sports and music of "the good old days," they are sharing common experiences, just as women do when we talk about ourselves: our parents, our old boyfriends, first dates, and other fiascoes. Through these "personal" anecdotes, women realize that we have all had the same childhood. Men must feel the same way when they talk about the 1979 Super Bowl or the 1984 World Series: we've all been there; we know. No matter whether you are male or female, talk, including gossip, makes us aware of our common ground. It establishes a sense of community. Maybe that's the best defense I have for my love of gossip.

Telling the truth is never as easy as I once assumed it was. I do feel guilty, though, when I fail to tell the truth in some major way. My Japanese friends and I were not brought up to lie on all occasions. What we received was a very mixed message: lying is all right under some circumstances, and yet honesty is also very important.

Honesty was especially important when it was linked with the idea of respect. We were taught never to lie to our teachers, parents, or elders. If we did anything wrong at school or at home, we had to own up to it as soon as possible. Being respectful to our elders meant being honest with them. Even our names reflected these values. The names of the Kuzuha brothers, Makoto and Tadashi, are two versions or connotations of "honesty": Makoto means "sincerity" and Tadashi means "correctness." My name and my brother's are two forms of "respect": my name means a reverent kind of respect, while his refers to the peaceful feeling of humility. So when our two families went on trips together and the four of us were playing on the beach or in the field, we were meant to be four embodiments of respect and honesty.

From our names and from the stories we heard, we did learn a certain reverence for the truth. One of the scariest images of my childhood comes from the Buddhist belief about the liars' hell. Buddhist folklore has different types of hell for different sins and vices, and many of the stories were told to us children to make us behave. If we didn't eat all our rice, we might end up in "the hungry goblins' hell," where people were tormented with hunger: they wandered around barren fields and mountains for eternity, looking for food and finding none, all because they didn't finish their bowls of rice in their lifetime. When grown-ups—usually my grandmother or neighborhood old ladies—told us this story, I laughed. "What about people who didn't finish their carrots or eggs?" I would ask. "Why is the story always about rice? What about bread? Would we have to go to the hungry goblins' hell if we cut off the crust to make sandwiches?" My grandmother and the other old ladies would shake their heads and say that I had missed the point of the story, and I would laugh some more. "But I already know the point of the story. You want me to eat all my rice."

The one hell that truly scared me was the liars' hell. We were told that the liars' hell is ruled by a king, En-ma-san, who keeps track of all the lies we have ever told in our life-time. When we die, we must stand before this king, who brings out a scroll in which all our lies are written down. He reads the scroll and decides if we are liars or not. If En-ma-san decides that we are liars, he makes us approach his throne and tells us to open our mouths so he can cut off our tongues. This story, unlike the others, did not involve wan-dering around or burning or drowning for eternity; the pun-ishment was a single event, making it sound as though we were free to go and do whatever we liked once our tongues were cut off. All the same, the liars' hell was the worst kind of hell. Without my tongue, I would never be able to talk or taste my food. The people in the other hells were heard screaming and yelling while they burned or drowned or were stabbed. At least they could talk, if only to curse their fate.

A few years ago at a museum in New Orleans, I was walk-ing through the Asian collection when I saw a small wooden statue about a foot tall: an old man seated on a throne with a frown on his face, as though he were perpetually chiding us. The card underneath said, "En-ma: the king of hell." De-cades away from my childhood, I stood staring at this statue as if I were seeing an old relative I did not like. Almost all the other statues in the room were bodhisattvas—gaunt, androgynous, and tall, their slender arms stretched out in gestures of forgiveness and mercy. They seemed utterly forgettable. Even though the bodhisattvas were five, ten times the size of En-ma, they were already shrinking in my memory while the old man, with his slight slouch, looked as though he were preparing to stand up from his throne and follow me home.

He has, in a way. I still picture him now and then—especially after telling polite lies because I lack the courage to tell the truth. En-ma-san sits in a dark room, frowning, slouching, and writing down my lies. Near his throne, pink tongues lie in a pile, some of them still moving, as certain types of raw fish are said to wiggle in a gourmet's mouth. Like strange delicacies, the tongues are arranged on a plate— morbid pink petals I stare at and cannot stop.

SAFETY

⌗

From Green Bay, a trip to a major city—Milwaukee, Chicago, or Minneapolis—means two to five hours of driving through the countryside and small towns across Wisconsin, Illinois, or Minnesota. Although I like to travel, I sometimes worry about driving. I imagine that my car is making strange noises or that my tires look low. There is plenty of bad weather in all seasons: snow, heavy rain, lightning, fog, extreme cold. Then there is my bad sense of direction. About every thirty miles, I have a moment of panic: maybe I missed an important turn-off and am now heading in the wrong direction.

Unlike most of my friends in Wisconsin, I didn't learn to drive until I was twenty-seven. I still feel a little unsure about certain maneuvers, like parallel parking, which way the wheels should be turned when I'm parked on a hill, or what I should do if the car begins to skid in a snowstorm. Step-by-step instructions always confuse me. If this happens, then do this, but if that other thing happens, then you must do the second thing, unless there is also the third factor—and you must decide in five seconds exactly which situation you are dealing with and what should be done. I hate the combination of logic and pressure. It puts me back in the world of math problems I could never solve.

My fear isn't primarily about driving and logic, though. I don't hear my car making strange noises, or imagine myself skidding in snow, or worry about my tires blowing out, once I am within ten miles of the city. As soon as I can make out the distant skyline, I am relieved. Weather doesn't look quite as intimidating in big cities. Open space makes rain, fog, or lightning seem bigger: a wide-open sky full of disaster. Even though I get lost in cities as well as in the countryside, I know that I can go to a gas station and ask for directions. I don't have to imagine myself walking up to a farmhouse and being bitten by a pack of big dogs. If my car were to break down in any city, I would know if I was in a safe neighborhood—in which case I would walk to a pay phone—or not—in which case I would wait in my car for help. What I am really afraid of is not my car but the countryside, where everything looks the same and there may be no pay phones for twenty miles.

Mine is a typical city-person's fear of the countryside. Walking down Michigan Avenue in Chicago, I notice that I am breathing much easier than I was while driving across Wisconsin and Illinois to get there. Although I have come to feel comfortable enough in Green Bay, every time I visit Milwaukee or Chicago, I realize that I feel truly at home only in big cities. A small town isn't exactly like the countryside:

there are gas stations and grocery stores in a town of three hundred people, and Green Bay isn't even a very small town like that—it's a city with its own suburbs. Still, I miss the anonymity of a large city. If I get out of my car and walk across a parking lot in a small town or in parts of Green Bay, people can see me for miles. Almost no one walks in the Midwest except in big cities; elsewhere, everyone knows everyone and can recognize one another's car or winter coat from a few blocks away, so any stranger sticks out. I feel much safer in big cities as I cross the street in a crowd and weave my way through the canyonlike gaps between buildings. Nobody notices me or cares who I am. The sense of security I feel is physical. As soon as I see the tall buildings and the crowd and the cars, I feel surrounded rather than exposed. It's similar to the way I prefer to sleep under a sheet even on the hottest summer day. I like a little protective layer between me and the ceiling, between me and whatever is out there.

Maybe we are all like the city mouse and the country mouse of our childhood fables. No matter which we come from, a big city, a small town, or the countryside, life seems easier in the kind of setting we knew as a child. My friends who come from rural Wisconsin worry about having their cars break down when they go to big cities, though they don't hesitate to drive the same cars across a hundred miles of countryside to visit their parents. Both my Japanese friends from Tokyo and my American friends from New York would feel more at home in Paris or Berlin than in a small fishing village on the Sea of Japan or in Stevens Point, Wisconsin. "What would I eat in a small town like that?" they worry. "Where would I stay? What if I didn't have any cash and all the banks were closed?"

We gravitate toward the settings we associate with home. I feel safe in big cities, not because I underestimate the crime rate, but because I know how to interpret what I see. A bad neighborhood looks like a bad neighborhood, in ways that I cannot explain to someone who doesn't know. When I stop at a gas station because I am lost, I can tell whether this is the kind of place where I should park my car two feet from the door, run into the store, and ask the attendant for directions—or where I should get some gas, saunter into the store to buy a soda, and ask to use the bathroom. For someone who is afraid of big cities, all busy streets look equally threatening—just as all farmhouses look, to me, like places where a person would be bitten by big dogs.

While my sense of safety is influenced by my childhood familiarity with big cities, in an odd way I don't feel as safe in Japan as everyone else seems to. I know how safe Japanese cities are, and yet I can never relax.

My relatives and friends feel as safe among strangers as among their close friends. When my aunt, my brother, and I got on a crowded commuter train in Osaka, she closed her eyes as soon as she sat down in the only seat that was open. All around her, people were standing shoulder to shoulder, their swaying bodies looming over her. Crammed against her narrow green seat, the side of her arm touching another woman's, my aunt dozed. She wasn't alone. At least half the passengers were sleeping. Businessmen in their dark suits were nodding and brushing against one another's heads and shoulders, snoring comfortably together on their way to work. Many people had their eyes closed while standing up.

Surrounded by all the sleeping people, I gripped the handrail, trying to stand straight. Every couple of minutes, the train swayed sideways, pitching me against other people's shoulders and hips. *How can these people sleep in public?* I wondered. Outside the windows, the dark green pines and cedars whipped by. The train rattled on, tossing the sleepers back and forth against one another. There was no privacy, and no one cared. Maybe people who did not grow up in Japan would witness this scene and think, *How wonderful. Japanese people are like a big family. They can sleep on trains, trusting that no one will steal their money or harm them.* But the scene made me feel closed in and afraid. When I sleep, dreaming about long-ago memories or some anxious event from the day before, I want to be alone. Sleep is intimate and personal—not something I want to share with strangers. Watching the others, I felt oppressed by what seemed like forced closeness or trust.

For me, crowded trains are the ultimate metaphor for Japanese society. Standing or sitting shoulder to shoulder, people sleep together, and yet they won't make eye contact or start casual conversations. There is a forced closeness that doesn't lead to true intimacy, communication, or even contact. Trains are also models of punctuality and orderliness—the high standard of Japanese discipline I was taught in grade school and rebelled against. Even more than that, I associate the trains with the period of my life when I was afraid of everything.

Many people say that they were fearless to the point of stupidity in their teens and early twenties. They attended wild parties and drove home drunk at dawn. "I did all kinds of stupid things," they say, now in their thirties or forties, "because I was too young to be afraid. I never thought anything bad could happen to me. I was lucky that I didn't get hurt." They attribute their former daring to "stupidity," "a false sense of immortality," or having no family to look after. They are more cautious now, they claim, because they are smarter and have more responsibilities.

That isn't how it was for me. I am much more relaxed and daring now than I used to be as a teenager. I still am not the kind of person who wants to jump out of airplanes, drive race cars, or get wildly drunk, but I can, if I have to, drive my car in a blizzard, confront someone who is angry or drunk, or come home at three in the morning and walk across a deserted parking lot to a dark apartment. I am not fearless, but I can overcome most unreasonable fears and act in a reasonable way: I am not afraid of everything the way I used to be as a teenager in a perfectly "safe" suburb in Japan.

One of the things I feared most at that time was coming home late at night. When I was eighteen, I taught English at a language school in Osaka two nights a week. After the class got out, I rushed to the station to catch the nine-fifteen train. Most nights, there were only one or two men in every car. From their black suits and white shirts, I knew that they were businessmen coming home from a late night at the office or from a drinking session with co-workers. I entered the car quietly and sat as far away from them as possible. Almost always, they were either sleeping or reading; their expressionless faces gave me the chills, especially if they were reading *Manga*—pornographic comic books that feature stories about women being raped, tortured, or murdered. Many businessmen read *Manga* on the train, and I had never heard of anyone assaulting women in real life because he had read these books. The men I saw on the train did not leer at me or look at me; still, I felt nervous and uncomfortable, knowing that they were looking at pictures of tied-up, naked women as we rode the same train.

When the train arrived in Ashiya, I ran to the cab stand outside to get in line. My neighborhood was supposed to be safe, and yet I was afraid to walk home in the dark. Once in a while, my friends and I heard stories about girls who had been raped while walking alone late at night. Girls like that lost their reputation. Even if they came from rich families who might try to keep the incident a secret, people always found out. These girls were marked for life. No matter how well they behaved for the rest of their lives, they would never be considered respectable enough to marry or have a good job. "What was she doing, walking late at night by herself like that?" people would always say about her.

But I was afraid of taking a cab, too. Getting into the back seat, I would mumble the address and the directions, my heart already beating faster. I sat bolt upright, as close to the door as I could, afraid of the silent cabdriver with his expressionless face—who could say that he was not going to turn out to be a murderer or a rapist? As the cab followed the familiar way home, I would relax about the driver, only to worry about getting home too late and being beaten by my father. My father and stepmother never gave me a specific curfew. Yet when I got home, my father might come to the door and hit me in the face for staying out too late, or he might be angry because my stepmother had complained to him about something I'd said or done.

There was no telling, every night, what I might find once I got home.

I was afraid of everything, I understand now, because I felt so unprotected. If anything happened to me outside the home, people would assume it was my own fault. The whole society would dismiss me forever as a girl who had invited disaster by her own careless conduct. My friends, who had to be careful outside the home for the same reason, at least had a safe place to return to. My home was no sanctuary. I had no one to take care of me, to worry about me in the protective way my friends' mothers did. If I was hurt by a stranger, my father and stepmother would be the first to blame me.

In my memory of those years, I am always taking the late-night train by myself. There is nothing between me and the dark streets outside except the fragile sheet of window glass. Trapped inside the train with businessmen—and their S&M fantasies—I am hurrying home toward people who won't hesitate to hurt me.

On my last visit to Tokyo, I decided it was time to overcome my bad feelings about trains. I rode the subway to various neighborhoods I'd never visited before and was impressed by the convenience and the punctuality of the system. Though I was in Tokyo only a few months after the members of the Aum cult had released sarin gas on a crowded subway train, I did not worry about being poisoned, any more than I worry about airplane crashes and other catastrophes that are statistically unlikely to befall me.

But something happened on the trip to undermine my sense of security. One Sunday, I decided to take a train to Kamakura, a suburb about an hour from Tokyo. The trains that go to suburbs have their seats arranged so four people can sit together, two each on opposite seats. Getting on the train, I took one of the few open seats, next to an old woman. Mine was the aisle seat and hers was the window. In typical Japanese fashion, she politely moved closer to the window to give me more room but said nothing. Avoiding eye contact, she craned her neck sideways to look out the window.

As the train started moving, I leaned back a little, trying not to stare at anyone or make rude eye contact. The seat facing me was occupied by two people. A woman my age was sleeping, leaning toward the window; she was wearing a brown kimono. Next to her—directly opposite me—sat a man in his late forties or fifties, wearing a white polo shirt and black pants. The woman and the man, I concluded, were not together—she was sitting as far away from him as possible, and also, they were dressed too differently to be going to the same place. To avoid staring at them and being intrusive, I looked out the window for a while, but the old woman's head was in the way so I couldn't see anything, and it seemed silly or maybe rude to be staring at the back of her head.

I turned back from the window and for the first time noticed that the man opposite me was scratching his crotch through his black pants. Embarrassed, I looked away. Even with my face turned away, I could not help but notice that he never stopped scratching, that his hand was moving up and down from his upper thigh, over his crotch, and then down again in a circular motion. When he noticed that I had noticed, he narrowed his eyes and leered. His gaze moved slowly from my legs, up my body, to my face, then back down. Next to him, the woman in the kimono continued to sleep; next to me, the old woman was still looking out the window, her upper body turned away from me. I could not tell whether the two women were really unaware of what was going on or if they were pretending not to notice. Maybe I was imagining this whole thing, I thought—surely, no one would sleep while a man masturbated right next to her. All I had to do was shift my eyes a slight amount to see him staring at me and touching himself while the woman in the kimono dozed, her eyes closed and her mouth open.

I did not confront the man or call the two women's attention to what was going on. I did not even get up to find a different seat right away. I sat immobilized, averting my eyes. The two women's unawareness added to my confusion and embarrassment. I felt that I was supposed to say nothing, to stay calm, and to do nothing until the train stopped. To disturb anyone—to embarrass them—was unthinkable. At the next station, I got up and walked to a different car. I looked back just in time to see the man get up and move in the opposite direction. He wasn't getting off the train, which was moving again—he was going to a different car, for all I know, to masturbate in front of someone else.

As I sat down in my new seat, my heart was pounding. I glanced around me quickly to make sure that the man did not change his mind and decide to follow me. The car I was in looked just like the one I had left, crowded with sleeping men and women. The man had not followed me.

I took a deep breath and closed my eyes, but I could not relax.

The worst part of the incident was everyone's silence, including—and especially—my own. Someone had masturbated right in front of me, using my body and my presence in a way that was absolutely degrading, and all I worried about was not causing a rude disturbance to the other passengers. I couldn't get over the feeling of shame—I felt as though the whole thing was my fault somehow. For a few days, I was too embarrassed to talk about it. When I did, I found out that "minor" sexual assaults happen all the time on trains. A woman who lived in Tokyo all her life said that when she was in high school, on a late-night train, a man stood in front of her and began to masturbate.

"I was pretty young," she said, "so I didn't know what was going on at first. There were only two or three other people in the car. The girl who had been sitting next to me got up suddenly and left as soon as the man came over. I thought, 'What a rude girl. Why doesn't she want to sit next to me?' Obviously, the other girl had realized what was about to happen. In a few minutes, I understood, too. I got up and walked to the next car."

This woman didn't seem to consider the event to be a particularly traumatic one. The man did not try to grab her as she stood up or follow her. She considered his actions to be offensive rather than threatening. But masturbating in front of someone is a form of sexual assault—the act is not simply distasteful but wrong and abusive. I was disturbed to hear that "minor sexual incidents" happen all the time on trains: men masturbating in front of women or even fondling their breasts and never being reported, much less apprehended. Women don't talk about these incidents except to their close friends, and for the most part, they shrug and agree that weird men on trains are a source of nuisance— something they have to live with and not think about too much.

I continue to feel unsafe in Japan because of the way women are embarrassed or pressured into silence. I am afraid, not so much because of the "weird men" on trains, but because of the silence. My silence is my own fault. After just a few days in Japan, I lose whatever assertiveness or courage I learned as an adult; much of what I hoped was my adult "character" or "principle" is just the luxury of living elsewhere. If I lived in Japan, it wouldn't take me long to accept and practice the polite silence everyone resorts to. That's what I fear the most—a community of enforced silence, and the ease with which that kind of community can crush most people's personal courage or assertiveness.

In Japan, polite communal silence assumes or implies a sense of safety—a woman sleeping on the train while her seatmate masturbates. She is supposed to stay quiet and not disturb the public peace because she is assumed to be in no "real" danger from the man. But not all situations that call for silence in Japan are so "harmless." Sometimes, there are actual physical dangers, and still no one says anything.

While I was in Tokyo, I heard about a woman whose former boyfriend had threatened her.

"The guy came to her apartment at midnight," a close friend of hers—a man I met on business—told me. "He pounded on the door and yelled at her. She told him to go away. He broke down the door, picked up her fire extinguisher, and sprayed foam into the doorway. Then he kept verbally abusing her. He didn't hit her or physically harm her, but she was quite shaken. He said that he would come back again—that's a threat, so she went to the police." The man shook his head and sighed. "But the police were no good. They sided with the boyfriend and accused her of being a loose woman. The policeman who interviewed her asked many personal questions about her love life, all the time staring at her chest. He claimed that since she didn't own her apartment, the damage her boyfriend caused was against her landlord, not against her—because of this, the policeman said, she would not be able to press charges. She went home in tears and called me."

"What did you tell her?" I asked him.

"I didn't know what to say. I gave her the number of the counselors at the Tokyo Women's Center. She hasn't called them yet." The Women's Center is a private organization that has various programs to help women.

"Can't she go back to the police station and report this policeman to his supervisor?" I asked.

"No. Policemen always stick together. She's afraid of getting on the wrong side of them. If she does, then she won't have anyone to call if the guy comes back again. My friend wishes that she had never gone to the police. She was humiliated to be asked all these questions about her sexual history and to be told that she was a loose woman. 'What do you expect?' the policeman said to her. 'No wonder your lover got angry. You should have been more upright.' "

The man who told me the story was afraid that the

Women's Center could do only so much, being a private organization with limited funds. People in Japan don't hire attorneys to take one another—much less the police—to court. What his friend experienced was a fairly common occurrence.

"The best solution for her," he said, "is to go to the media. The media are usually sympathetic to the plight of women. But I'm not sure if she can stand the publicity."

I am not naive about the police in the States. Like everyone else who owns a TV set, I saw the videotape of the police beating Rodney King, and I am disturbed by reported incidents of police brutality, racism, or incompetence. But in the small and safe town where I live, I certainly do not expect the police to beat me up if I were stopped for speeding. I would be shocked if a police officer scolded me or stared at my chest while I was reporting a crime.

I did once report a crime to the Green Bay police. A few years ago someone stole Chuck's guitars from our living room because we didn't lock the garage door. The two police "detectives" who came when we called 911 were pretty unhelpful: they came back two weeks later and showed us pictures of right-handed guitars and asked Chuck if those might be his—we had specifically told them that his were custom-made left-handed models. The police never found the guitars or caught the thieves. But they did not scold us for having failed to lock the garage door. If they had, we would have been outraged—even though it *was* our fault that we hadn't locked the door.

It didn't take us too long to get over whatever bad feelings we had about the theft. The "crime" didn't make us feel unsafe in our house. The thieves took nothing else and apparently had no intention of harming us or our cat. We talked rather flippantly about how our house was the site of the only crime that had taken place in our neighborhood in the last thirty years—after a while, the incident became one of our favorite anecdotes. But if we had been discouraged from talking about the incident or told that the theft had been our own fault, it would have been a different story: we would have felt unsafe.

The key to all my fears is silence. I feel uneasy in Japan because we are supposed to say nothing about whatever threatens our safety: from perverts on trains to family abuse or midnight break-ins by old boyfriends. Behind the smooth and quiet surface, I sense danger. The well-groomed businessmen on late-night trains, their heads bent over sadomasochism comic books, are emblematic of everything I fear in Japan. Even though they are most likely harmless to me, I can never be sure. I do not understand how someone could read violent and misogynous fantasies and still remain calm, polite, well-groomed, perfectly "nice." The silent, smooth surface is what gives me the creeps.

My fear of the countryside also has to do with silence. Out on a rural highway, I am afraid of the quiet. If something happened to me, no one would hear me or come to help me. I'm made uneasy by the sense of isolation or the lack of communication—the great distance to the nearest pay phone or the gas station. I am uncomfortable with the seemingly peaceful and friendly atmosphere because I associate it with the smooth and polite surface of life in Japan. When everything looks peaceful and no one talks, my guard goes up.

In the city, there is always noise. Everywhere I go, there are crowds of people—maybe not all of them mean well by me, but I am willing to take my chances. In most American cities, danger isn't hidden behind smooth surfaces or polite silences. To me, noise is a relief. At least it gives me a chance to join in and make my own noise, whether to express my opinion or to call for help. In a noisy American city, I feel safe from the oppressive silence of my past.

HOME

❊

Getting on the plane to leave Japan at the end of my trip is like boarding a time machine. The moment I take my seat, everything that happened in the last week falls into the distant past. From the small window of the plane, the observation decks and the gates of the airport look far away, as though I were seeing them through binoculars. That's how the whole trip strikes me as soon as I'm on the plane: small, far away, detailed. Like the migratory birds I watch through my binoculars, Japan becomes something for me to observe, study, recall.

I am jolted by the sudden shift of perspective. During my stay in Kobe, I feel as though I had never really left my childhood home. "I'll be here again soon," I say to my relatives and friends. "We'll always be in touch." Vaguely I imagine myself spending more time in Kobe in the future, by teaching a semester at a Japanese university or applying for a grant, and seeing my uncles, aunts, and cousins regularly for a while. If I had a teaching job, I reason, maybe living in Japan would not make me feel so helpless and scared: a job would remind me that I am a full, functioning adult; it would give me a chance to know Japan from a different perspective, and I could finally become more than an occasional visitor to my family.

Sitting on the plane and remembering these thoughts, I wonder, *What was I thinking? There's no way I could stay there for more than a couple of weeks. Who was I trying to fool?* As the plane begins to taxi and then to lift off into the sky, I am relieved. I *got out of there in time*, I think, *Thank goodness*. Up in the air, it's easy to admit the truth: it will be a long time before I am in Japan again, on another short visit; until then, I will think of my family and friends often, but they won't know because I won't write or call. This truth fills me with regret. I wish things had turned out a different way—it would be so nice if I could live my adult life without leaving behind my past in a foreign country—but a wish is only a wish: a strong feeling that does not affect the course of my life or the choices I make.

Due to the prevailing winds, the trip back from Japan to the United States is a couple of hours shorter than the trip the other way. From Tokyo or Osaka, I fly into San Francisco, go through the immigration and customs lines there, and then continue on to Detroit, where I board another plane to Green Bay. Each time I change planes, there are fewer Japanese or Asian people on board. On my first plane from Japan, I am surrounded by Japanese tourists. All the English announcements are followed by Japanese translations. As I fall in and out of sleep during the nine-hour flight, I hear the people around me talking to one another in Japanese.

On the plane to Detroit, there are only a few other Asians or Asian-Americans—business people traveling alone. The Japanese tourists, who travel in tour groups or with family members, have dispersed, and the bilingual announcements have stopped. All the same, I find myself waking up from sleep, thinking that the people around me are speaking in Japanese. I look around, only to find a blond and blue-eyed family of four, with a baby and a toddler. Awake, I hear the mother say to one of the kids, "Do you want some juice?" I doze off again and wake up, this time thinking that I hear my aunt and cousin speaking somewhere in the back of the plane. Behind me, there are fifteen, twenty rows of passengers, most of them asleep or reading in the narrow cone of light from the overhead reading lamp. Nobody is speaking, in any language.

As the plane speeds toward the Midwest, I recall the promises I made to my family and friends about coming back soon to visit. Even though I wanted the promises to be more than polite remarks, they can't be anything else. It doesn't do any good to wish that things had turned out differently. I am a balloon cut off and floating away into the blue sky. I have nothing to hold me anchored to the country of my birth, and yet I feel out of place among people who look nothing like me.

Ten, twenty minutes away from Detroit, the seatbelt sign goes on, and the plane begins to lose altitude. My ears ringing, I close my eyes and feel us tipping to the right, then to the left. People begin to wake up or put away their books;

they are collecting their belongings and pulling out their tickets to review their connecting flights. In the general buzz of conversation behind me, I can no longer hear the Japanese phrases. With my eyes closed, I wish I could fall back to sleep and hear my aunts' and friends' voices again. I feel nostalgic for the things I was—and am—so willing to leave behind. Just for five, ten more minutes until landing, I want to hear the voices of the past, its familiar intonations, the vague and endless apologies.

The contradictory emotions I feel are nothing unusual. Most of my friends experience the same feelings when they visit their parents' home in another city or another state. During the visit, they feel as though they had never left home, but as soon as they drive away or board the plane, the week they just spent "back home" seems more a part of their lives from twenty years ago than a recent event in their present life. "Was I really helping my father with his lawn this morning, or was it twenty years ago before I went to college?" they wonder as they travel back to their present homes—already making plans for the classes they will teach on Monday or reminding themselves that tomorrow is their daughter's first soccer game of the season. The week "back home" with their parents seems oddly out of place and time. The visit is a trip across time as well as distance.

When people ask me how I could leave my "home" at twenty and never go back, I remind them that there is nothing unusual about my choice. Many people leave home at eighteen to go to college and end up settling in another state, perhaps across the continent. They don't write, call, or visit their original families much more than I do. Or else people move to the next suburb only three miles away and yet feel a dissonance when they go "home" on holidays, because they have traveled a long distance from their parents' politics or religion. It's not so difficult to leave your "home" at eighteen or twenty, when you think of it as a place you were born to, not a place you have chosen. It didn't require any special courage for me to leave behind everything I loved about my home at twenty. There was very little I loved about Kobe back then. I was eager to leave the house where I never felt safe, much less "at home," and the culture that did not value intelligent and independent women—the kind of woman I wanted to become.

When I miss home now, it is the place itself I miss more than anything. At least once every month in my dreams, I stand on a seashore looking at a blue stretch of salt water, knowing that I am home. The dream may start out in another part of my home town: the busy downtown shopping district, my grade school up on the hill. Or it may begin some place far away. I am driving across the bridge on a country road in Wisconsin. Below me, there is an ice-covered river, and ahead, another long expanse of bare, brown fields. I turn the next corner, and suddenly, I am face to face with the salt water of my childhood.

The landscapes of childhood are imprinted on our memory. Many of us, miles, oceans, and years away from our first homes, return to them in our dreams. Chuck keeps dreaming about the only busy intersection with four-way stops that was in the small town where he went to kindergarten. In the dream, he may be walking on Seventh Avenue in New York, but when he crosses the street, he will find himself standing at the old intersection with an A&W behind him, a Mobil station ahead, and a grain mill down the street to the right. All new places, perhaps, point us back home.

Kobe is a city built on a narrow strip of land between the mountains and the sea. No matter where you are in the city, you can see the mountains to the north or the sea to the south. When people in Kobe give directions, they don't say *kita* (north) and *minami* (south); they say *yamagawa* (mountain side) and *umigawa* (sea side), even if they are in the middle of town, a few miles from either the mountains or the sea. I once took a cab in Kobe with three people from a publishing company in Tokyo. The cab driver asked us if the building we wanted to go to was on the sea side of the train station. A woman from Tokyo said, "No. The building is only a block from the station. It's not near the sea." "He means south," I told her as though she did not speak the language and I were her interpreter.

Landscape is more potent than culture. Even though the people from Tokyo had lived in Japan all their lives, they were like foreigners in Kobe. Tokyo is built on a flat plain. To people who grew up there, the mountains of Kobe must look overwhelming. All three of them kept squinting as they looked north, as though they could not quite believe what they saw. They were surprised to meet old men and women walking up and down the steep hills that are everywhere in the city. Though I had not lived in Kobe for eighteen years, I felt completely at home.

But the familiarity with childhood landscapes is only one way to feel at home. Happy as I am to see the mountains and the sea on my trips back "home," I begin to feel restless after only a few hours there. As I gaze at the mountains and the sea or sit down to dinner with my family and friends, time goes into slow motion. Moments seem like lifetimes, and I want to live them as though nothing else mattered, but deep down I know this is not my life, that my real life happens far away from my childhood landscape.

We mean so many things by home. Kobe would still be my home if home simply meant the place where we grew up, a place that is special to us because of our memories. But home also means a place where we have made a life for ourselves, where we feel a sense of purpose. I have never held a full-time job, voted, or paid taxes in Kobe, never supported a political cause or donated money or volunteered my time to help other people there. I could never call a place home without doing some of these things—without feeling that I have a part to play in the community. I left Japan because there was nothing for me to do there. I could get married and try to become an exemplary mother and wife, or live alone to pursue a career in isolation. Neither of these choices offers the kind of community involvement I find fulfilling: to have my own life and yet to be part of a larger life, a web of friends and like-minded people.

I don't regret leaving, but as a result, I have two halves of the whole when it comes to home—home as a special place of childhood, home as a place where I can live, work, be part of the community, and feel happy. The two halves don't make a smooth whole. Driving through the endlessly flat landscapes of the Midwest, I long for the mountains and the sea, the dramatic rise and fall of land and water around me. Like most people who grew up near any sea, I stare at Midwesterners with polite disbelief when they tell me that the

Great Lakes are like the ocean. Nobody who grew up near salt water would say that. I am always lonely for a home where I can have everything: the past, the present, the future.

Still, I believe that there is another way to come home. A few years ago, on my first visit to Cleveland, Ohio, I stood in front of the paintings by van Gogh, Monet, Renoir, Cézanne, and Bonnard in the Impressionist wing of the museum. I felt oddly at home: I had stood in front of some of these paintings at different times, in different cities—going back decades to the first traveling Impressionist exhibits I saw with my mother in Kyoto when I was eight. Thirty years later, I was standing, again, in the same space: six inches away from the canvas, the space my mother and I had occupied for a few seconds on a cloudy day in Kyoto. I felt comforted by the familiar paintings, just as I felt comforted by the familiar landscapes of Kobe.

This sense of home has little to do with actual places. The Impressionists painted places I have never seen in my life: the gardens of Giverny, the bridges over the Seine, the rail works and gray cobblestones of Paris. All the same, these were the images my mother had loved and taught me to love: Bonnard's white explosion of apple blossoms, Monet's blurred light on water lilies.

Art brings me home. Walking through the various museums all over America, I walk in the beauty my mother taught me to love. I stand between Monet's wisterias and van Gogh's irises and think of the gardens my mother planted, the letters she wrote home, telling her parents when the peonies bloomed, when we picked the first strawberries. Like paintings and gardens, words, letters, and books, too, can bring me home.

I grew up reading an assortment of British and American

novels. My favorite books between ages eight and twenty were: *Emily of New Moon, Little Women, The Secret Garden, The Catcher in the Rye, Jane Eyre, Pride and Prejudice, Tess of the d'Urbervilles.* Returning to these books, authors, or similar books and authors now, I feel a sense of homecoming. Last winter, in bed with a flu, I started Edith Wharton's *The Age of Innocence.* Only a few pages into the book, I was struck by a sense of familiarity. I recognized the ironic voice of the narrator. I knew the leisurely pace of the first scene. Already, I anticipated the slow unfolding of the story, which I knew would gain momentum and become a page-turner. I was back in the world of my favorite nineteenth- and early twentieth-century authors: Austen, Eliot, Hardy, Trollope. I was home.

Looking back at my favorite books, I notice that few of the main characters have a home they can take for granted. Jane Eyre and Emily Starr are orphans. The Bennett sisters in *Pride and Prejudice* know that the home they grew up in will belong to a distant cousin after their father's death; unless they marry, they will be homeless. In *The Catcher in the Rye*, Holden Caulfield briefly comes home, only to hide in the closet, worry about the ducks in Central Park, and give his sister the broken pieces of a record. Holden wants desperately to come home, if not to his parents' apartment, then to the rye field where he can catch the falling kids. It doesn't matter that his dream is based on the lyrics of a childhood song he remembers imperfectly.

Holden's rye field is very much like my sense of home: an imagined place that brings together the comforting elements of childhood. For Holden, these elements are the remembered song, the dreamlike images of other children, and an urge to love and protect them. For me, the sense of home brings together the paintings and the books my mother taught me to love. Cézanne's pears and the robins and ivy of *The Secret Garden* connect my childhood home to the home I have made in Wisconsin, where I look yearly for the return of the migratory birds and the blossoming of wildflowers. I keep coming home to books just as my dreams bring me back to the expanse of blue water.

Living in and between two cultures, I am often more confused than helped by the lessons I learned or rebelled against in both places. The question of home will always make me feel a little anxious and edgy. Often, when I meet people at academic conferences and tell them where I live, they laugh a little and say, "Really?" as though there was something incongruous about me—a Japanese woman from Kobe—making my home in Green Bay, Wisconsin. Perhaps these people are right. If I could move my job and my close friends, my whole adult life, somewhere else, I would choose to live in Milwaukee or Chicago. Ten years ago, if someone had asked me to name my ideal city, I would have said New York or San Francisco, or even Albuquerque. I've settled into a life in the Midwest. I love the easy pace of life, even the all-pervasive "niceness" I used to make fun of a long time ago: a place like Green Bay allows my friends and me to put together a living without much effort, to do whatever we want among people who are too nice not to let us be. So I don't long for the coasts or even for better weather. Some days I still miss a childhood place where everything seemed clear and simple—north meant the mountains and south meant the sea—but I know that this place is more mythical than actual. The past doesn't have all the answers.

In spite of my mother's love, my childhood home was a place of sadness, secrets, and lies. My mother's unhappiness with her life, a life that included me, is one of the hard truths I have to face. Love isn't always enough to keep someone alive or to pull her out of unhappiness. My mother chose to die rather than to practice the Japanese virtue of gaman in hopes of a better future with me. I know she would be pleased with my attempt to be honest about that. My mother spent most of her adult life trying to live a polite lie of a stable and harmonious marriage, trying, day after day, to make the lie become the truth somehow; her death meant a final rejection of that lie. If there was one thing she wanted me to do, it was to resist the polite lies and the silences of my childhood, to speak the truth.

The last conversation my mother and I had, when I was twelve, was over the phone. Somehow, that has made it easier for me to imagine her voice even after her death, even in a foreign country. I picture invisible telephone wires stretching over the ocean, across that immense gap of time I travel into my childhood on my visits to Japan. My mother's voice continues to reach me across that distance and time. The summer I left home, I stood looking at the waves coming in to San Francisco Bay and knew that in a roundabout way, the same water moved back and forth across the world—it didn't matter where I was. I had left home, I was sure, not to forget about my mother but to be closer to her memory. All these years later, my conviction remains the same: I speak her words though I speak them in another language.

© Katherine McCabe

ABOUT THE AUTHOR

KYOKO MORI's award-winning first novel, *Shizuko's Daughter*, was hailed by the *New York Times* as "a jewel of a book, one of those rarities that shine out only a few times in a generation." Now that her books have been published in translation in Japan, magazines and newspapers there frequently ask her to "interpret" America for the Japanese and to comment on the roles of women in the two countries. Kyoko Mori teaches creative writing at St. Norbert's College in De Pere, Wisconsin.

Look for this stirring memoir by Kyoko Mori

THE DREAM OF WATER

A Memoir

"AFFECTING...POIGNANT...Written in spare, shimmering prose that illuminates images and emotions." —*The New York Times Book Review*

KYOKO MORI
AUTHOR OF *SHIZUKO'S DAUGHTER*

"AFFECTING ... POIGNANT ... Written in spare, shimmering prose that illuminates images and emotions."
The New York Times Book Review

In an extraordinary memoir that is both a search for belonging and a search for understanding, Japanese-American author Kyoko Mori travels back to Kobe, Japan, the city of her birth, in an unspoken desire to come to terms with the memory of her mother's suicide and the family she left behind thirteen years before....

"POETIC ... REMARKABLY HONEST ...
Mori describes her experiences with an admirable mixture of forthrightness and restraint."
The Wall Street Journal

Available in bookstores everywhere.
Published by One World/Ballantine Books
The Ballantine Publishing Group
www.randomhouse.com/BB/

And look for her NEW YORK TIMES Notable Book, which was also a PUBLISHERS WEEKLY Best Book of the Year

"A JEWEL OF A BOOK, ONE OF THOSE RARITIES THAT SHINE ONLY A FEW TIMES IN A GENERATION . . . A WORK OF ART."
The New York Times Book Review

"Your mother would be very proud. . . ." Yuki Okuda heard these words when she was achieving in school, excelling in sports, even when she became president of the Kobe student council. And she could always imagine the unexpressed thought that followed: ". . . if your mother hadn't killed herself."

But Shizuko Okuda did commit suicide, and Yuki had to learn how to live with a father who didn't seem to love her and a stepmother who treated her badly. Most important, she had to learn how to live with herself: a twelve-year-old Japanese girl growing up alone, trying to make sense of a tragedy that made no sense at all. . . .